THE WORLD IS
A HUGE MARKET PLACE !

Are we ready for it ?

THE PERFECT SALESMAN?

. . . .

How do we get there?

Mr. Dieter Luloh

CHAPTER 1

· ·

The Beginning!

Once we are born, we start to sell our selves. When we see the light of life, the first thing we are doing, is crying. We want somebody to know, that we are cold and miss our warm surroundings. We offer somebody to take care of us and as it usually comes, either the mother or somebody close to her, raps us into a warm blanket. -We made a sale.-

From then on, throughout our lives, we always sell something. When we get older and we would like a toy, that we had seen somewhere, we have to go to mom or pop and try to convince them, that we are worthy to get that toy. Either we do it in a nice manner, or we try to black mail our parents. (" Mom, if you get me that toy, I will be a nice boy!") Or we charm our mom by giving her all attention, with a cute little face until we get our toy. When we get older, now we can talk, and try to convince them that we absolutely need a bigger toy. Here again, we are selling our selves once more. If your Mom or dad likes the way you approached them and you get that toy, you made a sale.

Growing further into life, we are approaching a world, that lives from sales. Our lives are totally depending on merchandize that is being offered to us and we need those. We have to buy them, to live a civilest life.

Now we have a choice, to buy the necessary things from more than one source. The first thing, we hope to find a sales person, who knows how to deal with us. Many times, there will be no sale, because we didn't like the approach of this sales person. What was he or she doing wrong? We don't know. It just didn't feel right.

To be in a professional sales atmosphere, whether or not you will be a good sales person, is mostly determent by our genes. We all know, that all our behavior and the way we act, is initiated by them. That doesn't mean, that the one who has not the right gene, cannot be a good sales person. It becomes only harder for him, because she or he has to control their natural behavior. To fake to be different, is very hard to do. You have to be a very good actor to project that to your customer.

At my younger adult life, I did a lot of different things, and everything I did, had to do with selling myself to somebody, to get a job or a girl friend, without really being aware of it. With everything I did, I was quite successful. Later in my life, I figured, that I must have a couple of good genes.

Growing more into my life, at one point I was approached by a friend of mine, that told me, that he is leaving a sales job with a furniture company and he asked me, if I would be interested to take his job. In spite of being a little frightened of all the people that I had to see, to make sales, I told him, that I would be interested. In the meantime, I had married and started a family.

At the first introduction to my new company, the sales manager noticed my coyness and after talking for a long time, he told me, that he was willing to give me a trial. Even though, I only was paid on commission base, I took the job.

The time we lived in was a few years after the war in Germany, where I was born, and the industry had not evolved to its capacity. There were hardly any furniture stores. So, the company came out with a beautiful printed catalog, where you could see only one piece of furniture, printed on a single page throughout the whole catalog The advertising was done via magazines and news papers. The readers than could send in a pre-printed return postcard with their name and address. I than had to go to them and set up a appointment, for a good time to see them at their convenience. There were not too many telephones at that time, so I had to do everything with my little car.

Once I had set up a date, mostly at the later hours in the day and over the weekend, I had to show three catalogs to them, and they could take all the time in the world to go through them. One guarantee we had to give to our company was, not to leave those catalogs alone with the customer. Sometimes this rule was hard to explain to the people. The reason for that was, that, when the customer had questions, that we were there to answer them right away, and of course to get a order right there. It was always important, when you set down with your customers, to find a place for yourself, that was slightly higher, than the rest of the family. This has a psychological effect. It puts you in a higher position, because you look down to the people, which gives you a feeling of being in control. The people on the other hand had to look up to you and sees in you, the man in control. In some cases, I left the people alone with my catalogs, because I felt, I had to do that, to make them comfortable in making a decision, as to what piece the wanted to buy. The most powerful information I could give them was, that the furniture they were buying was brand new and nobody else ever laid a hand on them.

Even though, I never felt comfortable in my sales position, because of lack of confidence in myself, but I was always very proud, to have made a good a sale. A good sale meant, that, when the customer signed the papers, for us to make sure, he was happy about it. An unsecure customer, could mean a lot of problems later on.

On one of the annual sales meetings that were arranged by my company, always one person was announced as the salesman of the year, by adding up his sales amounts during the last year. The next year, the same salesman was called again and I noticed, among all these people, I was sitting right behind him. When I looked at him, I also noticed how commonly he was dressed. I had expected a good looking and modern dressed sales representative. Because I always made sure, that I was dressed properly. On one of the breaks we had, I approached him and started to ask him some questions about his sales methods. After a while, he took me away from the crowd and asked me, if I tried to copy his way of selling. I kind of said yes, and here is what he told me: " Never try to imitate somebody else. Be yourself, because people will notice if you are faking it." I never forgot this advice in my whole life.

At that time, I was looking into the mirror and asked myself : " Am I the right person to be in this profession?" After talking to my wife and to our family, I got the confirmation, that I have what I need, to be a good salesman. With that in my mind, I hit the market with a new attitude. In the following years, I never became number one salesman, but I did o.k. for me and my family.

After a few years, my company was dissolved, because the competition was growing. Many furniture stores had opened and had their furniture on display.

When one day a friend of mine, told me, that there was gas station for lease on the market. Since I had a lot of interest in cars, I applied for it and got it. I was very excited to know, that I now would learn, how to blend in with the public.

Now I found out very quickly, that all my sales experience was not helping me selling our products. Besides offering gasoline, I was permitted only to change the oil and wash cars. The very negative side of all this was, that the gas I sold, was of the highest quality and was mostly used for high powered and very expensive cars, and I had to charge the highest gas prices. However, I was surrounded by six lower priced stations and even my best sales skills were ignored. However, in spite of all my efforts, I could not manage to live on the sales I made. I became very depressed, because I thought this was my fault. But life goes on.

So, at that time I had a chance to start a new job as an outside sales-man for a smokers paraphernalia wholesaler. When I met the owner and his wife, they explained to me, that they needed somebody to visit their customers, that he had set up about 30 years ago. In the meantime, her husband had taken a well paid job with a tobacco company not too far away from where they lived. During his absence his wife and a helper had tried to keep this company open. By now, that was over 20 years. But over that period, time had changed and companies sent their people out to see the customers directly.

CHAPTER 2

· ·

Progress!

To my delight, they had a fairly good looking station wagon ready to go with me. It was in the month of February and the weather in Germany at that time was mostly lousy.

The first week, the owner took a few days of vacation from his job and accompanied me on my first trip to some of his established customers. To be able to introduce new items we had for sale, he gave me three large suit cases with samples inside. Not only was it inconvenient to carry these into the store, but most of the stores he had set up were kind of small. Ones I had set and opened the cases, most of the floor space was covered. So when unfortunately a customer came in to the store, we had a hard time to arrange some space for him. So on the upcoming weekend, I took the old list of Customers set up 20 years ago and tried to organize it accordingly to city and streets. It took me two full days to do that.

The following Monday I was ready to go and felt good, because I had built a base, according to my new list. On this Monday morning it was very cloudy and it was raining. I had cleaned my company car, was dressed accordingly, had the three demo suitcases nicely stacked, and started up to go and see my first name on my list. After about an hour, I arrived in the City, where the customer was listed. I noticed, that most of the buildings were new. When I finally saw the right street number, I looked for a convenient parking space. When I finally found one, I took two of my cases and started to go back to the number I had seen. It was still raining and by the time, I arrived at that store, I was not only totally wet but the sign at the window of that store, showed a different name and a different display. When I walked to the inside, I was told, that the business I was asking for, was re-located to a different part of the city.

Very disappointed I took my two cases and walked back to my car, made a mark behind the name and concentrated on the next stop.

When I found it, I made sure, that the store had the right number and the right display. I saw everything in order and found a parking space not too far away. I took my two cases again and walked to that new store. It was still raining. When I got there and worked my way to the counter, I was looked at by two people. They watched me to get organized with my cases. The room was not very big, and when I introduced myself and the company I was working for, they treated me friendly and were surprised to see a representative from this company, that had never made contact to them in the last twenty years. After I explained the circumstances, they were very polite and looked at my cases and the display. I became very excited and I asked them to excuse me for a minute, went back to my car and got the third case. When I came back to the store, the people looked surprised. I opened the third case and noticed, there was no more ground space left. And to make this situation worse, a customer wanted to come in. When he saw what happened, he called his order across the room and I helped the woman to extend her arm to the customer to give him his order. Nobody was really happy about this situation and the store owner told me to pack my three cases. Of course they noticed my embarrassment, but they were nice enough to give me a small order.

By the time I had put all my cases in the back of my car, I was drenched and my moral was at the lowest. Not giving up, I tried to find the next address. I never found it, because the street was completely new arranged and as I found out, the store I was looking for, had gone out of business many years ago. Now I had lost my enthusiasm completely. Cursing the rain and the whole world of sales, I went back toward my home. On the way there, I stopped at my sister's house. She made me a nice cup of coffee and dried my hair with a towel and asked me, what happened.

After I told her, she looked at me and said: " My dear brother, I don't think, that sales is the right profession for you. You need to understand the system and the rejection that goes with it." I was happy for every word she said to me and gave her a big hug. When I told her, that I did not have another chance to get a good job in sales, because I had set all my future plans in being a salesman. We were at the fifth cup of coffee, she looked at me and ask me, if I wouldn't consider to join my brothers in America. Both of them were writing and telling me how happy they were to be in the States.. Until now, I ignored that, because I had a family with three girls, that were starting to grow into the German society.

I had always been a fan of the US. I was fascinated with their big cars and their lifestyle. Many times, when I saw an American car at the autobahn, I slowed down, drove behind them a while and just admired that car, that looked like a small bus.

Of course, all of the sudden, the idea to join my brothers in America, begun to bloom. When I came home that day very early and my wife asked me what's wrong, I told her about my disappointment. When I mentioned the idea to move to America, she looked at me like I was a ghost. It took her a while until she said: "What ?" To her, moving over there, was like somebody telling her to go to Mars. I didn't pursue this any further until we were in a more comfortable situation. When we calmly discussed my position and our future, she begun to understand, that for me, my chances to really become successful in Germany, had its borders. For somebody to really become successful, you needed a solid back ground of education. Since my time for that had come in a era, after the war, nothing was organized. There was no chance for me to find a functional company that was hiring young people to start a apprenticeship at any profession.

So, when we finally realized where we were standing, the idea with America was all of the sudden not so bad. I made some more contact with my brothers, who lived in Rockford, Illinois.

After I explained our situation, both of them agreed to do the best, to help me and my family to get over there. Of course, the next hard step was, to tell our parents. Even though her mother was strictly against it, I made all the preparations necessary to get it started. We came to the finale resolution, that I should go by myself first, to see what we could expect over there.

Talking to my brothers, they agreed with that and told me, that I could stay with one of them at his house as long as I needed.

With this plan, I booked a flight to the US on January the 2cond of 1969. That was only 2 months away. I was completely aware of the new circumstances that were waiting for me. Most of all that I could not speak the language. But my enthusiasm and my excitement helped me to get over that problem.

When we finally had finished talking to all our friends and members of our family, the time had come for me to say, let's go. So I boarded a propeller plane from Luxemburg to New York. My excitement held me back to sleep in the plane. After we made a landing in Iceland, to refuel, we arrived in New York the next morning at six o'clock. My travel arrangements, made with the help of my brothers, showed, that I had to take a bus to Chicago. After, with the help of the taxi driver, who spoke a little German, we located the Greyhound bus station in Manhattan. I stepped into a big hall, with all the gates and counters, to serve us. Except for a few pieces of paper, where one of my brothers had written something in English on one side and the translation of that in German on the other side. When I finally managed to get my bus ticket, I noticed, that I had two hours to kill before the bus left for Chicago. So, I took that chance and walked around 5th Ave, to get a first impression of my hopefully new country.

I was very much surprised and very excited what I saw. The picture of this city was so different from the pictures of cities I had seen in Europe. The wideness of the streets and the buildings and some cars that were long as a short train, were overwhelming. I couldn't see enough. Finally, when my time had come to go and catch my bus, I almost couldn't find my way back. Luckily I had remembered the Empire State Building, which was located next to the bus station, which was in sight from my present location.

CHAPTER 3

· ·

Expending!

Once I had figured the gate and the bus, I was happy, because so far nothing bad had happened. We took off on time and arrived on the outside of New York, We had killed 2 hours. Not familiar with the size of this country, I now begun to feel, how big everything here must be. When the darkness came over us, we had not even covered one fourth of the total distance. The people around me were all different and nobody was talking to anybody else. Giving in to my fate, I tried to get as comfortable as possible.

After a stop in Cleveland, Ohio, we finally arrived in Chicago six o'clock in the morning. Both of my brothers were waiting for me and were relieved, as I was, that we all could get to their respected homes and out of the cold, that had gripped the area, since a few days. The trip to their homes, took about an hour and was filled with a lively conversation. Of course, I was very tired. But I didn't mind that. I was just looking forward, to see what this country had in store for me. I was now thirty two years of age.

After a hearty welcome, I relaxed and really begun to crave for a bed. My sister in law had arranged for me to sleep in the room, that her oldest son occupied. I had a terrific night of sleep and felt pretty good when I got up the next morning. My brother had left to go to his Job and my sister in law set the table for a breakfast. This all was new for me. I had never had a breakfast that she had prepared for me. The table was half filled with food. It looked like, we were expecting more people. But when she came and filled my cup with coffee, I knew, this was a new country.

After a few days and a lot of conversation, which were often delayed, because most of it had to be translated from one language to the other, so everybody knew, what was talked about.

After I had notified my wife back in Germany and tried to settle down here in the States. I seriously begun to think and to talk to my brothers, about the reality to stay here. I loved everything I saw. My stay here was limited to six months in my passport. After a couple weeks later, we all agreed, that the chances for me looked very good. My oldest brother had lined up a job in a metalworking company, where he and I could be starting together, which would help me to communicate with my coworkers and our boss.

The first few weeks were very important to me. How could I get along with these new people. How did my new boss except me. Did I have a stable future for me and my family. But pretty soon I found out, that the American people that I had met, were very friendly and encouraged me to stay in their country. I had constant communication with my family in Germany. Even though my wife was not really in the mood to say "Yes", I kept telling her how great it was. I knew, she had to fight her mother, but after all, I was responsible for the future of my three girls and I didn't see any possibility to arrange our lives for the best, back at the old country. So, when I told her, that I wouldn't come back to Germany, she changed her mind and at my next phone call, she asked me what she had to do to come over. I gave instructions, and solved some problems with the immigration. She and my girls arrived in the US at the end of March. In the meantime I had to change the company where I worked, because the boss ran out orders. By this time, I was working at a big national food company, with an factory in Rockford. Here again, I had to sell myself a few times. In interviews with them, I tried my best and the people I talked to, excepted what I had to say and hired me. The sale was done.

Months had gone by, and my English had improved a bit., enough to communicate directly with the people. My wife and I rented a nice place to live, bought furniture and anything we needed to live comfortably.

We joined a German club and after a while, I noticed the different mentality between the two peoples. The longer I stayed in the US the more I moved over to the American side. We had met a lot of American families and were always welcome when we visited them. After about one year, we were able to buy a small house in a low income community. So I had a chance to meet very common people. I noticed their opinion about life, was a little different from anybody we had met before.

I took any chance to blend in with them and begun to understand, that America had a lot of negatives for a lot of people. But everybody was always very friendly when they saw us. My English got better and better. My kids went to the schools and wondered, why the people spoke so funny. After I explained to them, that we lived in a different country and that these people spoke a different language. It didn't take long and I saw them playing with our new neighbors.

In the meantime, I had applied for a green card to stay in the US. After my brother and I went to Chicago and talked to the emigration people, I got the permission to stay, after they noticed, that my brother was US citizen already for many years. That gave him the right to be joined by members of his family. The green card was valid for my whole family.

After a couple of years working as a mechanic at a food company, I was now capable of having a half way decent conversation with somebody. My kids spoke the language already without an accent.

When one day, my oldest brother came to me and told me, that he had a new job with a machine designer company for the metal working machinery.

This company needed a maintenance shop for their newly developed steel cutting saw. The prototype was delivered to a company in Wisconsin. I started with the new company and took a job as a driver to daily supply the company in Wisconsin with new tools. The new machine was supplied with up to 60 inch circular saw blades.

This job gave me a chance to go outside and meet people in their offices, which expanded my few of a big company's atmosphere. My goal still was to become a salesman someday. With my job as a driver, I never had the chance to talk to somebody important. But as it happened at one point the salesman of our company, ask me to take him to some leads he wanted to talk to. Many times I was able to listen in to some of his talks with a possible new customer. I noticed, that the conversation between them was very courteous.

Recalling some of my sales calls back in Germany, I was elated to be a witness of a sales conversation with a friendly atmosphere. Of course, I had a lot of questions to my salesman, who was often called Mr. Clean. He looked like that figure on TV, that offered a cleaning product.

A few years later, my brother was hired at a nationwide tool company, as the manager of their maintenance shop. This company signed a contract with a Swedish company, to import and sell their newly on the market coming special carbide tipped saw blades, that we had worked on at my previous company. This was a new step for them and they opened a independent branch, next to their headquarters in Wisconsin.

They also needed a salesman as well. Here was my chance. After a couple of interviews I was hired and had a big area to travel in and find customers for this new enterprise. After I was hired I asked the new manager, who was a younger man with a lot of energy, if my English was good enough to go out to get customers. He looked at me and said: " If they don't understand you, speak German with them." He laughed, turned around and walked away. They gave me a company car that was just the size, I always had admired in Germany. I felt like on top of the world.

The support I got from my young boss, gave me the necessary self insurance, I needed to become successful. Not only did I stop at my "old" customers, but also was eager to get new accounts.

I was lucky and in the next few weeks, I came back from my tours with a full trunk of tools that needed maintenance and new orders. Unfortunately, the shop had not had adequate time to be set up properly and the return of the tools to the customer took too long.

CHAPTER 4

. . . .

Growing Up in America!

I talked to my boss about that and he told me, that he would try to get everything in order. I don't know if he tried hard enough, but the circumstances did not improve. At one point, I had to asked for a new tire for my car, which was very much worn down, it took four weeks to get one. All this time I was taking a chance, to get a flat tire on one of the busy streets. I also noticed, that this company was working very slow to get anything done. My customers begun to complain about that.

Among all the new customers I had set up in the past weeks was a man, who came originally from the country of Lebanon. He had his own wholesale business with tools, that we sold. Thus, he became our customer. After a few visits from me, he involved me in a longer conversation and asked me about my background and my situation in my company. Because he also noticed the delay in tool delivery. When he noticed my disappointment in my answers, he made me an offer to become his salesman. Later on, when I thought about that, I started to compare the difference of the company I was working for now, which was a old established company, with a solid future and the new company that made me that offer, with a boss from a different country and no solid future. After discussing this situation with my wife, we came to the conclusion, that my future with that "old" company, was very much limited, since everything I was asking for, had to be decided by people, that had no idea what I was doing. So after only three months with my company, I talked to my young boss about my situation. He understood what I was saying and told me, that the things are, as they are. With other words, it would not change. So, with a strong hand shake and the return of my company car, which in the meantime had a new tire, he wished me good luck and if things wouldn't work out for me, I could knock on his door anytime.

Using my own car, I started as a independent salesman with the new company. I had a huge territory to cover. Included was Chicago and part of Wisconsin. Since I lived in Rockford, the distances were not too bad. Once a week, I had a meeting with my new boss and we allays discussed the coming week. Of course a lot of the customers I had with my previous company, stayed with me, so I had a good beginning.

However, after a few months of doing business for him, I notice some abnormalities. First of all, he did not have my weekly payment in time. The tools he had to sell for me, were not new. When I asked him about all that, he tried to deny the facts. Of course with an unstable background like this, I was not able to go out and make more sales. My disappointment was very visible. I had a hard time to face the facts and to admit to my wife, that I had made a bad decision to go with this man. (Later on in my life, I saw this as the first lesson in judging people.)

When I came home, I talked to my wife about this situation. Thinking back on that big company I worked for, didn't make me very happy. Because at that company my ambitions were limited. When one morning I got up and talked to my wife and asked her what opinion she had, if I would open up my own business. She left it up to me.

I was aware, that it was difficult, because I didn't have a shop to work on the tools, that I got back for service. Then I got a help from my brother, who was representing a German company, that sold the machines to service these tools. He told me, that he had just sold a machine to a small company, not too far away from where I had my customer base, and they might be interested to work with me. After I met them, we made an agreement to work together and I could bring in tools, that needed to be serviced.

At that time, I bought myself a Ford van and marked it with my new company name with big yellow letters. So, I visited all my customers and was lucky, that many of them stayed with me. After a time went by, I had picked up some of the biggest woodworking companies, located within the limits of Chicago. It didn't take too long and my competitors became aware of me. They tried to harm me, by telling the people all kinds of bad stories about me. However, I succeeded because my customers noticed, that the work I did, was of higher quality than what they got from the other service shops. So, after about a year, I was able to buy my own machines I needed for my purpose. I rented a small place in a small metalworking company.

From now on my life changed drastically. In the morning I had to visit my customers and returned the tools and in the afternoon I had to work in the shop to service the used tools. This was indeed a hard time for me and my family. After a while, I was able to get my own shop in the same neighborhood . In this period I met a lot of people. Among those was a Gentleman that represented a Swedish company, where I bought all my saw blades from. After about three years, this gentleman came to me and told me, that there was a German company, that came out with very modern machines for servicing those tools, and he was looking for a representative for his machines here in the US.

In the meantime my marriage had suffered not only because I was hardly home but also because the American lifestyle had changed our perspective to look at this new world. We divorced after a few months and stayed friends up to today.

This new offer looked very interested to me and after I had a chance to see these people in Germany and looked at their new machines. After we all liked each other, we set up a contract and I went home with a lot new good hopes in my heart.

When I came back, I talked to my people in the shop, and explained that new situation to them. Then, I looked for a bigger place and found one not too far away from my present shop. I split that building up in two half's and embellished the second half to make it nice looking for a show room

It didn't take too long and I got my first shipments of machines from Germany. After I had cleared them through the customs, I set them up in that new shop. Now the next obligation I had was to introduce these machines to the market. I had only one competitor in the US also selling machines made in Germany.

The next step was to book a booth at the national machine trade show in Louisville, Kentucky. But until then, it was a long time.

So I arranged a house show at my shop and sent out invitations to possible buyers. I also put advertising in all important magazines. The response was overwhelming. We all were looking forward to that show date. Once it arrived, I had a car standing by to pick up the visitors from the airport at O'Hare. A friend of mine declared himself as my driver. He did a good job and in no time, I had a lot of people in my showroom. I had prepared something to eat for them and had some German beer in the fridge. We all had a good time and when everything was over, I had some orders. This was a very good start. Not only had my machines a different structure, but I was considerably lower with my price.

The future looked very promising and when the time for the big show arrived, we were very excited. I had to spend a lot of money and all of that came out of my pocket, but I had high hopes and everything looked very promising.

With these new machines, I stirred up a lot of interest not only in the market but also from my competitor. Until now, he had no competition to speak of. At the next machine show, the representative from the company came over to my place and after looking for a while, he came to my booth and said: "You got something here." turned around and went to his booth, which was not too far away from the one I had.

By the end of the show, I gathered a lot of business cards, and when I came back to my office, I set up a plan to follow these leads. I decided to see them all in person. It took me a week and a half to see all of them. When I was done and came back to my office, I had exactly one order. This was another occasion, I had to learn a hard lesson. The vast majority of the people, that gave me a business card, were very small outfits. Some of them had a little shop in their basement and could not effort a machine to do a good job.

CHAPTER 5

. . . .

A new beginning!

Many others told me, that they were happy with what they got and others told me, they would "think" about it. From then on in my later sales life I was very careful to set too much hope on the business cards.

However, I concentrated on the bigger companies, because in the meantime, these newer tools from Europe came more and more into the market and the old time machines, that the shops were using, did not do the job to restore the tools to their original condition.

In the next few months, I got more and more calls and some of the people came to my place to take a closer look at my machines. So, I begun to write orders. A few weeks went by when I heard the news on the radio, that the American Dollar had lost its value against the German Mark. It was a big drop and to equal the Mark, I had to go up with my prices. I knew, that many of the customers that gave me an order and paid twenty percent down, had bought it, because of my price, compared to my competitor. Now another thing came to light: My competitor lowered his price to a lower level, than what I had. Since his machines were on the market all ready for a long time, and had a very good reputation, I could not compete with his price.

This was a very smart move of him, because he knew, that I was new on the market and figured that my financial supply was limited and therefore gave me a hard blow. He was right. When I called my customers, that had ordered a machine, that the price had gone up and topped the price of my competitor, they were asking for their money back. Of course I knew, that I had to comply with that, and therefore created another big problem. A new order of machines were already shipped and half way across the ocean. When

I informed the Germans about this new situation, they showed me the cold shoulder and told me, that this would be my problem.

Not being able to come up with all that money, I had to make a decision. I still hat my sharpening shop going and therefore I told the Germans, that I would take my machine business out of existents. Now it was their problem.

This choice was easy, because I had something to fall back on. During the following time, that I was thinking of getting a smaller place, I got a phone call from a gentleman located in Georgia. After he introduced himself, he told me, that he had seen me at the show in Kentucky and he was very impressed with my sales tactic. When he heard from somebody, that I had broken up with that German company, he wanted to know if I would be interested to sell his machines, that also served the woodworking industry. These machines were of much smaller size and were only manually to operate. They were made for smaller companies, that were located outside of the bigger cities, mostly family enterprises. My job was to follow leads that he created by advertising in trade magazines. To do this, he operated a special model of a Ford van, with a high top and a with carpets covered floor. Further, inside he had mounted three of his machines, surrounded by two smaller chairs and a modern stereo system. My travel area was not limited and I could work in the whole United States. Since I was single and had no one to hold me back, I agreed to take that job.

When I came back to my office, I arranged to sell my little shop to a company in Chicago. Once that was done, I flew over to Georgia and picked up the van. It was agreed, that I could make my planning for the trips from my location in Illinois.

I was very much surprised, that his advertising was so successful. The leads came in from all over the country. I was kind of excited about this, because it gave me a chance to get to know not only the different states, but also the different people. For the next two years I did a lot of traveling and wrote a lot of orders. On one occasion in the state of Idaho, I had a chance to meet and talk to a Chief of an Indian tribe. When he noticed that I was from Germany, he got me involved in a very interesting conversation. After two hours I was sad to break it up and had to leave. Of course after about one year, I had a pretty good idea how America was put together. In the south the people were different from the ones in the north or west. I also learned how to approach different people differently.

In the southern states I had a problem to be recognized because of the German accent I had maintained. Later on I found out, that even people coming from the north, were not always excepted. After another year, I moved to Georgia and took over the sales department.

Two years after I came to the States, a friend of mine took me to the movie "Deliverance". Even though I couldn't speak the language too well, I couldn't understand what the movie showed about those people in that part of the south. These mentally retarded people for me, were unreal. But I was assured, that these people actually existed. Later on, on one of my trips to the south, driving through some mountains together with a local dealer, he showed me some residences of these people were still living and he told me: "Don't ever stop here, even in case of a flat tire !"

In the meantime I had met a woman of my liking. She was also from Germany and worked at a insurance company in Chicago, her name was Edy and after a few years living together, I talked to her and her two kids about coming with me to Georgia. After just a little while, she agreed. When we got to Georgia I knew, I had met the right girl and asked her to marry me. We got married on the foot hills of the mountains in Georgia, at a German town and we had a great time with my boss and his wife.

Georgia was a very lovely state and we enjoyed to discover it more and more. A little while later, she started a job and her youngest daughter went to the local school. The older one joined a collage in Illinois.

Besides all the nice things we encountered in Georgia, we also noticed, that my boss, who's ethnic back ground was Irish, was very much depending on alcohol. I didn't noticed that before, because I hardly saw him when I lived in Illinois. Now in Georgia, I had to deal with him on a daily bases. The orders came in very nicely and at one point our warehouse was sold out.

When I didn't get new supplies and I asked him when we got the new machines, he told me that he didn't have enough money to buy new supplies, which mostly came from Taiwan. Here, I was in a peculiar situation again. This happened after about one year we had moved there. In the meantime, we found out, that we didn't belong there. We never felt comfortable with the people we had to live with.

So, when this new situation occurred, we were a little relieved, because now we a chance to move somewhere else. My boss in the meantime lost a court case and he moved to on other state up north west.

On all my travels I visited a company located in Tarpon Springs, Florida. Since this town is populated by Greeks, the owner of this business had immigrated from Greece a few years back, got married to a Greek woman which was born here in the states. With the help of his community, they opened up an woodworking shop.

On one of my trips to see them, he followed my demo of one of the machines I had in the van. He showed interest and it came to a sell. Later on he bought a second machine. We had a good relationship to each other and at one point, he asked me if I would be interested to take over a newly developed sales department in his neighborhood, owned by his cousin who was also from Greece. He was the owner of a import business, that was dealing with timber, coming from Columbia in South America. He owned a freighter and kept it busy with holing timber from over there and all kind of export goods to take to over there. He owned a big lot in town and had a lot of timber stored there.

In-between that timber he had built a office building, made completely from wood. He told me, that there is an opening for a sales manager.

Edy and I had been in Florida many times before and we always liked it. When my new situation came up I remembered that offer from the Greeks and made contact with them.

CHAPTER 6

My new life!

After I talked to him, he got very excited and told me, that he would contact his cousin immediately and he would let me know as soon as he talked to him. It didn't take too long and he called me and told me, that his cousin would like to see me as soon as possible. We made an appointment and I flew over there. After we met in this wooden office, he explained to me, that he had very good connections with some Brazilian companies, that were, together with the Germans, building the best woodworking machines in the world.

Now, according to my experiences in the past, he was right. The Germans were known to build a very reliable series of woodworking machines. They were the highest priced on the market. So if I could get those machines for less money, since they were made in Brazil, I would be in a good shape. After we settled the financial situation, he welcomed me to Florida.

My wife and I had no problem to pack everything we had in the hurry, took our youngest girl out of school, against her will, and moved to Clearwater, Florida, with a big truck. I drove the truck and my wife followed me in her car. All this didn't take more than three days.

On my last trip to Florida, I had arranged for a place to live. We got there on a Friday afternoon. That gave us some time to get settled. The following Monday I went to that wooden office, with all the timber around me. They gave me an office, that was actually occupied by another person. But I was told, that that person was out of the country and was not scheduled to come back soon. This office was supplied with an desk, a few shelves with paperwork in it and a telephone. From my position behind the desk, I had a view between the timber and a dog house. I noticed a few big dogs, with nothing to do, hanging around and looking at my office window.

I had my car parked at the front of the yard. next to was a repair shop for motor boats. A middle aged man was running that shop and I had a good understanding with him. He was always friendly. When the next day, I was informed to park my car within the yard, right next to my office. To do that, I had to drive all the way to the end of the yard, go around the repair shop and then to my office location. That was all o.k. until I got to my office location. When I tried to get out of the car, I had one of the big dogs standing in front of car door and looked at me very intensively but very quiet. I knew that behavior on dogs and my warning signal in my body started to come up.

Not to show my apprehension, I tried to open the door very slowly. The dog didn't move and kept on staring at me. I opened the door a little bit more and that dog turned into a wild beast. I was lucky to be able to pull the door back into the frame. The dog was jumping on my car, and was growling like a tiger. My window was smeared and the lower door was full of scratches. I was completely helpless. Lucky for me, my neighbor the repairman came and saw what was happening. Immediately he pulled the dog away from my car and took him to the dog pound and locked the steel door. It took me a while to calm down and to thank the man for helping me.

He explained to me, that the dogs had to see me more often, to get acquainted with me. From then on, it was a challenge for me every morning, to sneak by the dogs, that were released into the yard every night.

After I was used to that, I finally had a meeting with the owner, and after he apologist for the situation with the dogs, I asked him what he wanted me to do to get the business going. He explained to me again, the close connection he had with the Brazilians. He showed me a few of their flyers and explanation of their functioning. I was very familiar with these machines and was looking forward to get to the market with them.

From now on I was all by myself. All the flyers I had now were written in German. So what I did, translated all of these flyers into the American language, with a nice layout with pictures, so the American people could understand the purpose of these machines. This took me about a couple of weeks and I had them all in a pretty shape, printed by an professional printer shop.

The question was, how to introduce these Brazilian machines to the market. Besides the regular advertising, we had an offer from my old company, which had gone out of business, to take over the rented space in the upcoming machine show in Atlanta, Georgia, that they didn't need any more. The place was big enough, to show at least one of our big and one smaller machines. The time to that show was about four months away. So we had plenty of time to get organized. I talked this over with my boss and he told me to get those machines in time.

Time went by and we had some responses to our advertising. Since we were not known on the market, everybody I talked to, was happy to hear, that we were displaying two of those machines at the upcoming show in Atlanta. I was full of hopes and looked positive into the future. Everything seemed to be normal. There was one thing however, I found it a little strange, that I allays was paid in cash. Not losing any sleep over it, I was only paying attention to my job.

On one of my Florida trips, I was able to get an order from a young woodworking shop owner, who was convinced, that he was making a good deal with these machines. Because he knew about the reputation of the German. As it is usual, that he paid me a down payment with a check. When I came home with this order, everybody was ecstatic and looked at me, like I performed a miracle.

Speaking to more inquiries on the phone and preparing for the show, kept me busy. My wife had taken a job again with the same company, she had worked before. Since this company was a national enterprise, she could get a job there, where ever we lived.

The day of the show came closer and closer and we were under pressure to get that ordered machine into the US to get it to the show and afterwards to ship it to that customer. About three weeks before that show, I asked my boss, what the situation with the machines were. He made some phone calls and told me that the Brazilians had some problems with their government to export those machines to the US. They were on strike to make a point to them.

I was very worried and it came as it had come. We went to the show without the machines. We displayed timber pieces instead. We were quite successful with those and at least our show space was not wasted. After the show, I had to inform the customer, that bought the machine from me, that that machine could not be delivered. and I sent him his check back. From then on, my outlook to the future was dim. Every week, I was still paid in cash and at sometime, when nobody showed up to pay me on a payday, the lady came finally with the money later at night and counted the money out of a big suitcase. As I noticed, there was a lot of cash left in that case. Even though, she was very care full to open that case, but I saw it anyways.

That night, when I talked to my wife about it, we both didn't feel too good about it. On top of that, the younger Greek, that I had sold the two machines to, who was my bosses cousin, took me in his car and drove into the woods, to show me a big property, full of used woodworking machines. I was surprised to see that, because at one time, he told me, that the woodworking shop he was running, did not make enough profit to provide him with a comfortable life style.

Now putting everything together, I got a very funny feeling about all this and I begun to look for another job. I was right to do that, because a year later, when we lived in California, one night on all three main networks, It was announced and I saw it, that that company was besieged by the FBI and all the people inside, were arrested under the suspicion of smuggling tons of Cocaine into the USA. This drug was smuggled inside of the timber, he imported.

CHAPTER 7

· ·

Here we go again!

At the last machine show we had in Atlanta, I was approached by a owner of a very long established woodworking machine dealership, located in the city of Atlanta. I had met him a few times before and he hinted to me, that he would be interested to hire me as his representative in the state of Florida. Since I lived there now, I thought this would be a good change. I called him up and after a nice conversation. He was an elderly man and had founded his company more than thirty years ago.

As a young man, he had to leave Germany, because his parents were killed by the Nazi government. I had the entire state of Florida to represent his company. He had a mixture of woodworking machinery, most of them made in Germany. After all these years, working in the field of woodworkers, I was quite familiar with that equipment.

So I started with a secure feeling in me and it didn't take too long and I had my first orders. After a few weeks, I had the feeling, that Florida needed a experience salesman for the machines, because I had many interested customers in a short time. The advantage I had was first my experience and second, the German machines. They were known to be the most reliable. Even though, they were the highest priced, and sometimes I didn't get an order, because the customer just didn't have the financial support, but even when he bought a cheaper machine from another dealer, when it came to the point, that he needed a service for his machine and nobody showed up, I helped him to get that machine going.

So, in the long run, I got a good reputation among the woodworkers in Florida. The people at my company in Atlanta were kind of surprised and pretty soon, I had to wait to get a machine delivered, because their stock was very low.

After a couple of years I was informed by my boss, that he was selling the company to the German supplier of most of his machines. That did not make me happy. Since my experience with the German companies were everything but good. I had a lot of bad experiences with them in the past years. The reason for that was, that they had a hard time to adjust for the American market. Parts of their machines had to be replaced, with American parts, which they had a hard time to do.

It came as it had come again. When the Germans took over that office in Atlanta, the first thing they did, sent me a new business card with the wrong zip code. When I told them about that, to cover that mistake, they kind of let me know, that that was not important. I stayed with them until the next machine show in Atlanta. During the show, I was fully aware of the roll there were playing, to know everything better. I knew, that I would not get the support in the future, that I got from the old company and I especially when I notice, that they seem to like the American whiskey a little too much. I started to look for something else again.

It just happens, that in the city of Tampa, close to where I lived, was a woodworking supply company, that I had considered as my competitor, had been sold. The new owner was getting rid of the machine department and continued only with the supply of working materials. One of my customers called me up and told me, that that company is looking for a salesman, to sell out the machines, that they had left. I went over there and introduced myself. The new manager told me, that he knew about my reputation, and was happy to turn that department over to me. I started the next morning and noticed that they had a lot of machines, that were out of order. Machines, that were returned from their customers, because they were not made of a good quality and were returned to them.

First, I sorted out the good ones, made them presentable and offered these machines to the market. Since this company was well known all over the state, I had a bunch of customers coming in and take a look what I had to offer, especially because the prices that we announced, were attractively low.

So, it didn't take too long and had sold all the functioning machines in a matter of two weeks. I started to repair all the other machines. Calling in a lot of spare parts and making some changes, and after another few weeks I was sold out.

My wife, her daughter and I settled in Florida in the last few years and everybody had found a base for their lives. My wife's daughter had become a pretty teenager and had a lot of friends. Edy and I had begun to like Florida, by ignoring the terrible humidity. But now was time to re-group again. My job here was done and we had to look again for another opportunity, when on one day, I noticed an ad in a trade magazine, where a California company was looking for a regional sales rep, just outside of Los Angeles. It just happened, that I knew these people, which I had visited, when I was represented the Irish company outside of Atlanta. I knew, the people in California were young and had opened their company in a partnership. I talked to them on the phone, and we made an appointment to see them.

A few days later, I flew to them and they explained to me, what they had in mind. They were all together three people and had started that company three years ago, after they separated from the company, they had worked for, for many years. They were representing a few big accounts from Germany and were very successful. The area they had to cover, became too big for them and therefore thy needed one more salesman. One afternoon, one of them drove me through the area, that they had thought of to give to the new help. It was huge and had plenty of industry located inside.

Of course this new situation gave me and my wife a hard time to think. In our short past, we sometimes talked about California and always got ma little excited. So, when we had the chance to move there and if it would be only for a short time, we both agreed, it would be worth it. After all, we were still young and wanted to see as much of the world as we could.

So, we managed to sell all of our furniture except our bed, to our neighbors. I rented a trailer to fit our personal things in. At one day, after we had found a family, whose daughter was a close friend of my wife's younger daughter, that was happy to live with them in their house. They were both sixteen years old and my wife's daughter was not in the mood to come with us to California.

I understood her argument and told her, that she could stay in Florida. We knew the other people for a few years and trusted them with her.

The next Wednesday, early in the morning, we had loaded the trailer, we were all done and ready to go. When we slowly moved along the streets that we had lived on for the last few years, my car didn't seem to go very fast, until we were out of our area and were traveling lot faster.

I had never been traveling this far with a car. But we were in a good mood and nothing was too far for us, so we thought. Once we hit Hwy 10, it was practically all straight to California. The month we were driving now, was August. The humidity was awful and when we came into Louisiana, we were surprised by a very heavy storm and heavy rain. At one point I had the feeling, that my trailer was floating instead of rolling.

Staying overnight in Baton Rouge, the next morning was sunshine again. On our way to the west, we noticed, that the longer we were driving, the shorter the trees and bushes became. We crossed the border of Texas and half through Texas, we noticed, that the trees and bushes became taller again, but they looked different. The Humidity was gone and the drier air took over. Later in California we thought the leaves were made from plastic. They were brittle and dry. After another overnight stay, we thought, pretty soon to be in California. It seemed like our trip never came to an end.

When we finally got to our goal, the next thing we did was, stretching out in our hotel beds for the next hour.

CHAPTER 8

· ·

Challenging!

We didn't have a lot of time to relax, because the next morning, I had a meeting with my new company. This was a big party and many of the suppliers to that company, were also invited. The party was held outside at a swimming pool. The food and drink supply was plentiful. So, we had a good time. The next day Sunday we had some time to shop for furniture and other things we needed.

A few days later, we had another meeting in their office, to discuss the situation with the customers, that had been visited by one of the three owners of this company without any success for an order for a couple of years. The many business cards, that they had gathered from my area, were turned over to me, with an comment on each. On four of the cards, the comment was, not to bother to see them again, because they are not interested to buy anything new.

When I started to visit my future customers, I noticed, that the ones with the negative comments, were the biggest size of all. Starting with some smaller accounts, to get an opinion about the peoples attitude. I noticed, that the majority of the woodworkers were very alert and were eager to learn, what's new on the market. I also noticed, that they were skeptical toward machines, that were not built in their state.

Because California is big state, many of the woodworking machines were made there, but the quality, compared what was coming in from Europe, was very poor and very insufficient to run.

Finally I got some orders from some smaller places and after a few months, I had a pretty good idea, how to handle these people. So, at one point, I told myself to go to the biggies and to see, what they had to say.

The first one, not too far from where I lived, was a custom cutting enterprise, to cut big particle boards to pre- determent sizes. By walking to the office, I could tell, that they were very busy. They had three half automatic cutting saws, made in California, that needed seven people to operate. Immediately, I saw a possibility to lead a intelligent conversation.

When I was introduced to an elderly man, who was part owner of the company.

He invited me to sit down and started asking me all kind of questions. I liked that, when the customer started the conversation. That meant, that he was interested in me and to see where I came from and how much I knew about the woodworking industry and what I to offer. I didn't take too long and I found a niche, how to get close to him. I noticed a family picture on his side desk. Asking him, who that was, he grabbed the picture and explained to me what I wanted to know. We talked about one hour, without getting into business.

After we said bye for today, he invited me to stop in again. I promised him that and we parted as good aquatints. At another day, I came close to the second big customer. They were cutting boards out of solid wood trees.

Here again, the machine they were using, looked like it had come from Europe with Columbus. It was operated by foreigners, who had problems to say anything in English. When I went into the office, I met a very attractive, middle aged woman. She was very nicely dressed and greeted me very friendly. After we sat down and she asked me, why I was visiting her. I introduced myself properly and told her, that I was new in this area and I tried to get to know all the woodworkers that were located inside of it. She asked me what machines I was selling and I told her, that I could replace that old machine of hers for a new one, that would cut more wood four times faster with half of the people, that I saw were working on it now.

She looked at me and said: "Yes, I know that." When I asked her why she wouldn't go for it, she told me, that she is not the owner of this company, but she was in charge of all the operations. She also told me, that she had a big problem with the shop foreman and that he was a union man and on top of that he was German. Already he rejected all new equipment for the last few years. When I asked her, if it would be o.k. to try to meet this man, she nodded her head and said: "Good luck."

So I went across the yard and walked into the maintenance shop, where I saw two men doing something. I asked for his name the woman had given me and the older middle aged man turned to me and asked me what I wanted. I noticed his accent and I greeted him in German. He looked at me surprised. I stretched my hand to him and he shook it. After a little conversation in German, he got a little warmer and asked me where in Germany I was from and so in no time we had a nicer conversation going.

When I pointed to his old machine and asked him why he didn't want a new one, which was much easier to operate, he pulled a little back and told me, that he wasn't quite sure, if his boss would go along with that. When I told him, that the office woman sent me to him, he kind of looked away from me and I knew, there was something else he was fighting. Later, speaking with that woman again, she said, that it seems that that man was afraid, not to be able to handle that modern equipment. Knowing that, at a later day, I visited him again and started to tell him very carefully, how actually easy it was to learn how to handle it and if he would like me to take him to another customer, that was equipped with these new machines. After a while, I found out, that most of the people were afraid of the computers, that took over the control of the machine. To make it easy for them, I showed them a pocket calculator and asked them, if they would be able to work with this. Of course, nobody wanted to seem stupid by saying: "No" and so I told them, that the computer on the machines are just as easy to work with.

After a few days I got a phone call from that women. She told me, that this man had asked her to call me, to make an appointment to see a demonstration of this machine. Before I went to him, I made an appointment with one of the customers that had a complete set up of the machine he was interested on.

When I took him there and after I introduced him to the important people, I let him talk to the people only. They were on the same level that he was. In no time, I noticed that he got very focused on what the people showed him, to get involved with what that saw.

At this time, weeks had gone by, but finally I got an order from both of them, and even the third big company I was told not bother to sell anything, but I had visits a few times, warmed up to me and also gave me an order.

My office was very surprised to see that. But my selling method was different from the one, the indigenous people used. I was patient and sold myself first. So the people could built up their trust in me. I remembered the sentence

I had heard many years ago in Germany: "Make sure, when the customer signs the papers, he is content with it. An unsecure customer will always bother you with unimportant things." I always followed this motto in my future sales and most of the time, I was successful because after the customers got their machines, they saw, that everything I told them about what a machine could do for them, was true.

In this huge area, that all three of us covered, there were only a certain amount of companies, that were using these big machines and we had sold them all, and since these machines had the durability of ten to fifteen years, there was no repeat business to expect. From then on, I had to concentrate on the smaller outfits.

Among those were some small Chinese woodworking shops, that were located inside of their community, just outside of Los Angeles. At one point I received a lead from one of them trough my company.

When I went to this name and for the first time I saw a Chinese woodworking shop, I was quite shocked. Everything looked so primitive and out of order. The machines they were using were absolutely worth to send to a museum. I was surprised to see them working at all.

After I introduced myself to the owner, he was a middle aged skinny man and I had a hard time to understand him. Finally, after showing him my brochures of modern table saws, he saw the difference. With a smile on his face, he then started to talk about his country.

CHAPTER 9

· ·

The frightening future!

I showed him the necessary attention and even though, I understood only a fraction of what he said, we had developed a nice atmosphere. After about two hours, I asked him, if he liked the machine I showed him, he smiled again and nodded his head and in clear English, he said: "Yes", stood up, shook my hand to tell me: "Bye".

After a couple of more visits, just to say hello and get to know them a little better, when all of the sudden I got a phone call and a female Chinese voice told me, that her boss wanted to see me. When I got there, he had four more Chinese people around him and when he introduced me to them, it turned out that, each of them also owned of a woodworking shop. And low and behold, I got an order for one new machine from each. When all the machines were delivered and I had helped them to set them up and gave them proper training, I asked one of them, why they bought those machines from me, even though I had many of my competitors knocking on their doors. They told me, that I was the most patient salesman. Of course, this experience enriched my knowledge, how to deal with different people. At that time, I had no idea, how help full and important it really was for my future.

In the following weeks I kept visiting them and was able to write some more smaller orders. Mostly equipment that had to be attached to the machines.

My wife and I enjoyed California tremendously. Whenever we found free time for us, we went out there to explore new areas. On one side we had the snow covered mountains, on the other side we had the pacific ocean. The first one year, we were looking only for the nice things, blinded by our enthusiasm.

When the time of new discoveries was over, we begun to notice many negative things.

The first thing we were disappointed with, was the pollution of the beaches. At one point, we wanted to go swimming at the beach in Santa Monika, the water was so dirty, that we did not have the courage to go into it and that happened frequently.

From then on, we were more care full to make an comment about anything. Later on we heard on the TV, that some manure had returned from the ocean to the beach and the beaches were closed. On top of that, we were now suffering from the heavy air pollution. When I started to cough, my Doctor said: "Welcome to California." Edy had some problems with her breathing and took some medicine for it.

After about three years, we were not so fond of California any more, especially when one morning a nearby earthquake occurred. The epicenter laid in the town next door and hat a strength of 6.2. It was eight o'clock in the morning and at first I thought a heavy truck had passed by. But when I saw our heavy lamp, hanging from the top in our dining room, swinging back and forth very heavily, I realized that this was more than a truck. It was a earthquake. Edy and I got up in panic, because we were not prepared for that. I had experienced tornados and hurricanes, but there was always time to get into a safe place. But this earthquake was something, we couldn't deal with. Right after it was over, we had some bush fires around us and could not see the next house anymore. The time in California, in our minds, begun to run short. Besides all the local problems we encountered, we also noticed, that we were living very far away from the rest of our family. Some of our girls lived in Chicago and one in Florida. Finally one day, we had enough, sat down and weight the negatives against the positives. After we ended up with a lot of negatives and only one positive, (The sun was always shining), we looked at each other and four weeks later, after we had sold all of our furniture and everything else we had, we were in our loaded car and our compass was set to the east.

About a few months before all this happened, at a local machine show in Anaheim, I was approached by a man, with an heavy middle east accent and was asked, if I would be interested to work with him on a new laminate that came in from Europe. It was a German product, produced in Spain.

After the show was over, I went to see him in one of the suburbs of L.A. He had a small office with two rooms on top of a small store. The first room was supplied with a huge desk and a huge chair. The second room had everything smaller. After a very general conversation about that material, we set up another date.

After my call to him for an appointment, he had a younger man, also from the middle east, who spoke a lot better English, invited, to help him with his bad English. After we sat down, he started to explain, what he had to offer. The reason he had contacted me was, that he noticed my first name, which was typical German and he figured, that my German back ground, could help him to better communicate with the Germans.

I knew the woodworking industry very well and what I saw at his office, was indeed a new product. It was very flexible and could be used for just about anything. He could have something revolutionary here and after we cleared the price situation, we discussed my position in all this and came to the conclusion, that I was involved in negotiation with the Germans and the management in Spain. Of all the purchases, he had to pay me a certain percentage and he was responsible for my expenses I had on any of the trips I had to make. He announced me to the Germans and set up an appointment with the Spaniards at their head quarters in Balboa Spain. When that date came closer, I noticed that he had a hard time to come up with the money. He had no choice as to cancel that appointment. However, I was still interested in marketing this material. So, I made a call to the management in Spain and explained the situation with this man. I was happy to hear, that their representative, a Spanish man, was on his way to Canada to see their agent over there. Arrangements were made to meet me in L.A. We set a date and at that day I picked him up from the airport. He was a typical Spanish looking man, spoke perfectly German and English and two more languages. We stayed at the airport to talk, because his connecting flight was about four hours later. I noticed, that he was not a very patient man. I know through their history, the Spaniards were very proud people. I had a hard time to get on the same level with him.

At the end of our conversation, he agreed to work on a new set up in the US with me. So on my way to Chicago, I had a signed contract with his company, giving me the sole distribution right for marketing and selling of their Products here in the US.

After a few weeks, I got a shipment of samples as we agreed upon. Setting my marketing strategy in motion and was waiting for the response. I sent out letters to the individual woodworking shops and made calls to the in the US acting laminate distributors. The response I got was not bad. Among those was a owner of a woodworking shop in Florida. He had seen my letter and the flyer and he got very interested. When he called me one day, we had a long conversation. At this call, I gave him enough information, to get a good impression of our product.

After a few days, he called me again and we set up the conditions of him purchasing that product. They were: Pre-pay of the whole order including the freight costs from Spain. He agreed with that and a few days later, I got the money into my account. I was very proud of that, because I was able to win his trust for me.

I sent in the order and the money to Spain and got the confirmation for that. The delivery time was approximately four to six weeks. After one week he called me again and ask for the address and phone number of this company in Europe. The purpose of that was, for him to travel to Spain and see how that product was made. I thought at that moment, that that could strengthen our relationship.

My relationship with the company in Spain however was a little cool. When I had questions for them and I contacted them either by phone or in writing, it always took a long time for them to respond. At that time I figured, that was the Spanish style.

CHAPTER 10

. . . .

Honest business!

Another response to my advertising, was a owner of a woodworking shop in Ohio. After I called him, he was eager to come and see me and giving him a demonstration of my product.

A few days later, I met him at a hotel close to the toll way, that he had to use to come to me. I was waiting for him and after about twenty minutes, he came into the hotel lobby. When he saw me, he came over to me with an escort. He brought three extra coworkers with him, to make sure that what I had to offer was really something new.

He was an older man, but very quickly I knew, he was an expert in the woodworking era. In his shop, he laminated all kind of wooden moldings, that were installed into homes and offices. Right now he had no choice but to work with a American made laminate, which was very hard pressed and cracked very easily, thus, creating a lot of waste. When he saw and touched my material, he became ecstatic and discussed the possible work with it, with his escort. On the end of our meeting, he was a happy man and told me, that he would be interested in a partnership with me. For me this would be a good step, because he was the right type to communicate with the woodworkers all over this country.

After one week, I called me and told me that he had set up a appointment with an lawyer, to come to an agreement about a partnership. On the day that appointment was made, I had taken my wife with me and arrived one day before.

The time for the appointment was set for nine o'clock in the morning on a Monday. My future partner picked me up at the hotel and we drove to the location of the lawyers office This office was quite large and looked very comfortable. After we were all introduced, he instructed his secretary to make a new pot of coffee and invited us to sit down.

After I explained to the lawyer what my material was all about and a few powerful comments from my future partner, the lawyer all of the sudden showed a very private interest in our negotiations and after a few hours of talking back and forth he asked us if it would be possible to become a third partner in this matter. He said, that he was always looking to make a good investment in a promising matter.

We talked about this a little longer and came to the conclusion, that this new situation could help our new company. We settled for a name of the new company and declared the lawyer, at his request, the president. The arrangements were made and I had to move to Ohio, just outside of Cleveland. We set up a corporation and our president went to work right away. After all the papers were signed, he applied for a small business loan from the government, which was approved and there was nothing to hold us back. Immediately we ordered a container full of new products from Spain.

We had a good beginning. Time went by and I was surprised, that I hadn't heard from the man in Florida. After I had set up my office, I called him and encountered a very hostile voice from the man that used to be so happy to work with me. When I asked him how his trip went, he told me, that after he had met and talked to the management in Spain, the offered him to buy directly from their company in Spain for a price without my commission. I told him, that he couldn't do that because I had an exclusive contract with them. He was not concerned about that and told me, from now on he would be buying directly from them. When I contacted the man that made the contract with me, he did not react to that at all. I reported this to our president and also he was puzzled. We talked about this situation and came to the conclusion, to call the party in Florida and let him know, that we could get a restraining order to prevent for him to get the shipment. When he told us, that he had given the Spaniards a new order and had sent the money to them. After many more talks with him, we noticed, that he was not a wealthy man and his company was very small and he had only one helper to make enough money to support his family. The money he had sent to Spain was borrowed from a relative.

Since we had made quite a bit of investments and put in all the efforts to become a successful enterprise, and we got the promise from him not to go outside of Florida, we decided to let it go and give him a chance to make a decent living.

The next step was to get into the market, besides all the advertising we did, we also rented a space at the woodwork9ing show, held in Atlanta. Our woodworking partner, made a very good looking booth set up and when we got to Atlanta, we were happy to see, that our booth was located right next to a cafeteria. That meant, that a lot of people could see our display, while they had coffee and were relaxed.

The show was quite successful and also got the attention of our big competitors here in the states. At the show, I met some of my customers I had in California. They greeted me friendly and some of them regretted, that I was not with them anymore. That made me feel good.

After the show was over, we all sat together and worked very seriously on the leads, that were left with us. As the sales manager of our company, it was my responsibility to judge these leads as efficiently as I could. That I had learned from my past. Many intense phone calls sorted out the most promising and I made appointments with them. Since the names I got came from all over the country, I decided to take my car to visit them. It took me a few weeks to cover them all. After I was done with them, I had a very promising result. Four of the people that I had seen were ready to introduce our product to their customers. All of them were independent reps and had the freedom to take on another product. Another seven came out of the woodworking industry and wanted to go out with our product to set up a stabile base for their future. With these people, I was covering a nice part of the US.

To get everybody more acquainted with our product and our company, we invited all of them to come to a gathering at our town. All expenses paid.

All of them and a couple we didn't know of, applied for that. We set a date and some of them flew in or used their cars.

A week before, we had received our container order from Spain, so we had something to show for. But the main purpose of this gathering was actually to show these people how to work with this material. My woodworking partner did a very good job and everybody was very excited. Some of them still had a hangover from last night, but didn't miss any of the demonstrations. In the next few weeks, I accompanied all of these new people, when they visited their customers.

Even though, it was very hard to convince the American woodworkers, to take a closer look at this new commodity, some of them did and pretty soon we got some orders coming in. We were elated but noticed pretty soon it was very difficult to maintain a healthy stock. Since we sold much of a certain color, we ended up to face the fact, that we needed more materials. However, to get a nice discount from our supplier. we had to order a full container. Our money situation was still very limited, so we ordered only partial containers.

So, time went by and we worked as hard as we could, when one day, our president introduced me to a ex navy officer who was retired now and I was told, that he was a good friend of our president and that he had good possibilities to convince his ex partners at the navy to use our product to cover the walls of ships, that otherwise were painted with a gray paint, that everybody hated. So far they couldn't use any solid product to adhere to the walls, because of the vibration of the ship, that made the glue that was used to hold them to the wall, got brittle and released the wall covering. Since our material was very flexible, there was a chance it could withstand those vibrations.

Later, at one day, my president came to me and told me, that he got the o.k. from the navy, through his friend, to apply our material to a submarine supply ship, anchored in Norfolk Virginia. After we found out how much of our material we needed, we were ready to leave and to go to our ship. My woodworking partner had a pickup truck. We loaded it with everything we needed and took off.

CHAPTER 11

· ·

A new experience!

We left early in the morning and arrived at the navy yard in Norfolk in the late afternoon. We had a hard time to find that ship, because the war in Iraq had just begun and we were supposed to go through a security check, which was closed at this time. We had not reserved a hotel room, because we were told, that we could stay on board as long as we needed. In the meantime our ex navy man arrived with his son and two more people in his car. When I asked what these people were doing here, I was told one of them was a photographer, the other two were suppose to help us applying our material.

I was kind of nicely surprised and thought of our president as very thoughtful man. What I didn't know than, but what I found out pretty soon was, that all of this had to be paid by our company. That hit me in my stomach. Because on all my trips, I was very careful how to spend our company money. I stayed in the cheapest motels and made sure I didn't eat too expensive.

When we finally found the ship, we were guided up the gangway and lead to the officers meeting room. There we were informed, that we didn't get the clearance yet and therefore, we could not leave the ship until we were done with our job. We were then taken to our sleeping quarters which consisted of six beds in one room and two in another.

The space to walk between the beds was very small. The only privacy we had was a thin curtain in front of the beds that could be moved along the whole bed. For me, all this was an adventure and I sucked it in. We decided that my partner and I took the room with the two beds.

The next morning, we had a meeting with the commander of the ship. He instructed us how to behave as long as we were on board. We had to follow some certain rules, not only because the war was still going on, but also because we were on a ship, that accompanied a horde of nuclear submarines to service them as their supplier with all kind of weapons.

We were not suppose to take any pictures and were allowed to speak only with the crew, that was helping us with our job. We also were informed, that the next day they performed a drill on board, to "catch a thief." They pretended that somebody had stolen important papers from the captains room and they had to find out who did it.

The next day, when I took my stroll along the ship, all of the sudden, I was grabbed from behind and pushed against a wall, my arms were pulled to the back and I was asked who I was and what I was doing on board of this ship. Since I was wearing civil clothing, they thought they had caught the perpetrator. After a while of course they found out who I really was. For me however, that was a story to tell all my friends.

While several of our people were working on our order, I took a chance to walk around that ship. It was very interesting to see, how some things work at the navy. I could see some of the subs. Since we were also working on the reception room, the gangway, that was usually attached to it, was now mounted in the middle of the side of the ship. This gangway was only used for special purposes and was much longer than the original. Therefore, when you were half up, it begun to swing up and down and sideways. This position was for an civilian person, that was not used to it, very dangerous and many times I saw one of the guards running down to the people to help them.

Our work progressed and I enjoyed any minute being on this ship. After the third day, the captain came and looked what we had done to his information room and he was very happy about what he saw. He explained to me, that for him and most of the personal on board of any US ship, that the usual blue-ish color was not very exciting and made them sleepy. Our wall covering showed some trees and flowers and looked a lot friendlier. In fact he liked it so much, that he suggested to do the same with the submarines. Since those are very narrow, I had the chance to go and check it out. So, with an escort, I entered one of them and walked all the way to the end. I was overwhelmed to see, how stretched they are. I couldn't help it to get goose bumps all over my body.

After that visit, I let the captain know, that in some spaces it was possible. So, our retired navy officer an ex flyer with the "Hell Angels" group, got excited and assured to get a lot of orders out of that. We extended our work area to an extra room on land. This room was used by the Admiral and we selected the nicest covering for him. After we were all done we got a friendly "Good Bye" from all the people we had met there.

When we got home and we drew a conclusion out of what we had done over there, besides being the only company, that had a material, that could satisfy the navy, we had to come up with a lot of money, to satisfy our bank account.

Our president, the lawyer, was what his title said, a 'lawyer', but not a good business man. He just saw, that so far we had good money coming in, but it was not enough to go around and do big jobs for no charge. We still had to fight for a breakthrough into the market. Our competition, two large companies, controlled the whole market and they begun to advertise against us.

Since two of the leading members of our corporation used his own office for our company, we had two different offices on different locations. So, nobody knew what was going on in any of the offices. The president held the check book and all responsibilities as to the functioning of our company. At one point I was told, that our navy man was part of my sales department. After I talked to our president, he also told me, that we could expect a lot more orders from the navy and therefore he should have the authority to negotiate with the navy directly. On one hand this made sense, on the other I was asking myself, if he knew enough about our material, to really give them the right answers. Because I had seen many salesman over the years, that made false statements about their products, just to get an order. When later on they got problems, because they were not honest, they were nowhere to be found. My other partner and I agreed, that the course our company was taken, was not desirable.

CHAPTER 12

· ·

The old/new world!

Our president leaned more toward the navy to get orders, while I was pushing away from them and wanted to go our own ways.

This split between us lead to the day, when our navy man wanted to do more jobs for the navy for no charge. I objected to that and when I noticed, that our president actually went against me, I had enough and went home to my wife. It was two o'clock in the afternoon. She looked at me and of course noted my disappointment in my eyes. After a few seconds of quiet, she asked me: "What's the problem?" I sat down and said: "We are not going to make it." Of course, she knew about this already some time ago, but never mentioned anything. At that moment, I just looked at her and hugged her for a long time. The rest of that day, I didn't talk anymore.

The next morning she served coffee, she looked at me, but didn't say anything. I felt that look and asked her to sit down and also have a cup of coffee. After all, we all had spend a lot of time and effort over the last three years and all this went down, because a man, with a big title, that had no sales skills, started the down spiral of our company.

I saw myself at the end of the short stick again and got into a depression. I had done all I could and more and even we had a positive outlook for the future, we failed.

The next thing we did was, moving back to Chicago. I didn't talk to my partner again and knew, from now on, he had to carry all responsibilities. I didn't care what he was going to do with the company.

The last days in Ohio, I called my sister in Germany and explained the situation I was in. Here again, she spoke to me very calmly and asked me, if I would like to come back to Germany at least for a while until I had a normal outlook to the world again.

I knew, if I would do that, I would have to get a job in Germany. But being American citizen and the tight situation in the German job market, made me think very hard. My wife, still having the German citizenship, could be helpful.

After many more phone calls with my sister. and weighing all the chances I had or not had, we came to the conclusion, It would be a big help for me to get into a different atmosphere and at the same time, kill my homesickness for Germany. After discussing all this with our girls, we finally set a day to leave. Until then, we had time to sell our car and everything else.

The time came and our plane took us to Amsterdam. Sitting at that airport and waiting for the connecting flight to Germany, I felt like a man without a country. I always looked at my wife and she gave me always new hope. When we got to Germany, my sister had sent her youngest son to pick us up from the airport. When we came to her house, it was a big size with plenty of room, we were greeted and served with a good cup of coffee. Of course after all the time in the plane and at the airports, we both were dead tired and looked that way. After a short conversation, she showed us our room and it didn't take too long and we were asleep. Having had a good night, we were served a good breakfast and just knowing, I was far away from my troubles in the US, made me feel a lot better.

The house belonged to her husband's factory, that was right outside. He took over this enterprise, after his father turned it over to him a few years back.

After a few days, I started seriously to look for a job. An ad in the national paper did not give me anything. Local ads, the same. When one day my sisters son in-law came to me and told me, that he had made some contacts with a home center company he knew very well, and they were looking for a branch manager, located in my home town. I couldn't believe it.

After my introduction, and a long conversation, they said to call me in a few days. The days went by and really a got a phone call and they told me, that they were looking forward to give me proper training in preparation for the position as a branch manager.- I had sold myself again-.

After I got my work permit from the government, after all, I was American citizen, I started working at their headquarters, not too far away from I lived, and learned how the world of retail businesses was conducted in this country.

The first thing I noticed was, that the tone between the sales clerks and the customers was not very friendly. The explanation of a product to a customer was insufficient. I noticed that many of them were not satisfied with the answer they got and many times, they put the product back into the shelf.

Talking to my sisters family about that, they told me, that they knew about this. That's why the most people that spent some time in the US, agreed, that the friendliness in the US was much better than the one in Germany by a mile.

My first duties consisted of creating some layouts for future displays. After that time was over, I had to join the sales force. In the meantime, the general manager had called me in his office and he loved to talk about the American system. He told me to try to transfer some of my experience into their people, without letting them know. Of course everybody knew, that I came from the US. Teaching them was like straightening the tail of pig. It was just not their nature to be friendly.

At one point, I had a costumer with his wife, who was asking for a wall tile. We had some on display. Once they selected a particular pattern, I explained to them what the right way was to apply those tiles to the wall. I used my words very careful and loud enough to be heard by my collogues, and on the end, the customer thanked me and purchased everything I had suggested to them. We said a warm good bye and they parted as contend customers.

A few days went by and the same people came in again, to buy something else. When I saw them, I greeted them and asked them how it went with their job at home. They looked at me and with a friendly smile, they thanked me for my advice, and every time they came into our store, they came over to me and greeted me. That of course was very unusual and I had the attention of my bosses.

In the meantime, since I knew, we were going to move into my hometown, which was not far away, we were looking for a place to live.

Until now, we were still living with my sister and her family. When the day came, that I got my marching orders to my city, I was very relieved. Under very difficult circumstance, because at that time, there were no empty places, we were lucky and obtained a nice apartment just about in the middle of the city.

I started at my new location with my company as the assistant manager. My superior was a young woman, that had different plans for her future. Right from the beginning we had a friendly relationship. Besides the assistant manager position, I took over the wood department, which had been neglected for long time. The department next to me was headed by a young man from the neighbor town, who had just started with this company. His was head of the tool department and he his hands full to bring it up to date as well. Since we were so close together, we helped each other many times.

A few months later, after I cleaned and polished my department, my sales went up tremendously. Many of my customers I served once, came back over and over again. At one point, my department was declared the runner of our store. My young tool department boss and I started a friendship and kept a close relationship. When one day he came and told me, that he was quitting his job in this company to join a auto parts store, that he had worked at before and was more to his liking. However, we kept our friendship going.

A couple of years went by and my trust in me was restored.

CHAPTER 13

· ·

You are never too old to learn!

My wife, who really didn't like to live in Germany too much, right from the beginning, started looking at me and at one point she asked me, if we couldn't move back to the states. In the mean time, I had lost my home sickness for Germany and felt more home sickness for the US. After all, we had all our family living there.

After hard thinking and making some calls to some people in the US, we decided to do it. After all, all these years in Germany gave us a chance to be with our families. Edy's mother was still alive and so, I had a chance to meet her as well as her two brothers.

On one of my calls, to people in the US I knew, I was told by an salesman, that there was German company, that had come out with an small machine, that was designed to hold together any wooden frame, after it was cut. This was something new, because usually it took up to 24 hours in a special metal frame, to make the wood to stick to one another. I called these people in Germany and made an appointment. I took the train and was picked up by a son of the owner at the station.

When they showed me this machine, I knew this was something very new. One other son represented them in the US from a private house in Long Island. But the owner told me, he needed somebody else to expand that business all over the US. He hinted to me, that their youngest son was really not capable of doing that. Besides other weak points, he was there as a visitor and had to return to Germany every three months.

After a week, he called me and agreed with everything I was proposing to him. We notified my brother outside of Chicago and he agreed to give us shelter until we had found our own. I was very careful not to put all my trust in the Germans, since I had so many bad experiences with them before, but knowing the owner, who was a elderly man, engineer by trade, and looking very stable, I thought to give a chance.

When we got to the states, I had a written contract with him, saying that I was taking take over the distribution of his designed machines in the US.

Nesting in with my brother and his girlfriend, I left my wife with them when I had to go on a trip. After exhibiting our machines at a smaller show in Chicago, we had great interest from all kinds of people. Since one of the machines were designed for smaller companies, we had a lot of interest from them also. In fact, we got so may orders, that we ran out of stock within one week. The company started to fly them in from Germany, but their youngest son, who was not told, that I was supposed to take over that operation, started to screw up almost every order. When his dad called me and asked me why this was happening and I explained to him the situation, he talked to his son and let him know, that he is not in charge any more. His son than, locked all the doors on me and told me, that I was not working for them anymore.

At that time I was in Chicago and was using the company car that they had bought for me to use for the demonstration of the machines.

When I told his dad about this decision by his son, he told me to see him at the Chicago airport for a meeting with him. He gave me a date and at that day, I was waiting for him. in the car outside of the arrival terminal. When I saw him, I also noticed his son with him. Both of them came from Germany. We managed a cool hand shake and I drove to the next restaurant to have a cup of coffee and to listen to what he had to say. In the meantime, before this meeting, I had to go through more uncomfortable situations with his son and my enthusiasm was at the lowest level, because I saw myself in the middle of a family feud.

When we sat down and the coffee was served, the father wanted to know what happened. I was very careful not to separate these two people more. I told him with a few words, that I was not interested to be commanded by his son. When the son heard, from his dad, I was suppose to take over the his operation, he looked like, he was going to run out. Before he did that, I took the car keys and reached across the table with them, gave them to the father and told him, that I had no interest to work for him anymore. Of course their faces turned into a masks. I got up and told them good bye. Of course now, they had to drive to Long Island. I gave the directions and walked to my brothers house, which was not too far away.

It took me about ten minutes than we all sat down and had coffee. Now the question was, what's next.

The next morning, I was sitting outside and started to take a glance at the local paper. when I saw an ad that was looking for drivers at a limousine service about fifteen minutes away. My heart started to bounce a little higher, because for me to actually drive one of those big cars, would fulfill one of my dreams. Making a phone call to these people, I found out that there were no special abilities you had to have, to drive a limo. I talked it over with my family and at this time we all agreed, that any job was a good job, especially we needed to look for our own place to live.

I made an appointment with the limo company and the same after-noon I drove over to them. Approaching their property I saw a lot of limos parked there and I got really excited.

Once inside, I met the drivers manager. He invited me to come and sit down. After we cleared up my accent, he told me, to be able to drive for them, I had to go through a short trainings program and I needed a clean record of my past driving. A few seconds later, he checked my driving record and I was not surprised to see, that it was completely clean.

CHAPTER 14

. . . .

You are never too old to learn!

Just to get to know each other a little bit more, we carried on with an easy conversation. After a while, he told me, that I could start the next morning with my training, which I did.

When I got there, they had gathered eight more people. Later I found out, they had a lot of turn over's on drivers, because not everybody was cut out to be a good driver. That meant, you not only had to be a good driver, but also display good manners.

So, the training hour was gone by very fast and in the afternoon we were taken to the most likely places we had to take customers. Some of them were the airports and big companies.

Since we had some time between getting the order and actually picking up the people, we had to get the location from a local map. That required some skills, but after a while it was easy.

I was little disappointed, when my first car they gave me, was a regular passenger car size and had a few years on its odometer. The reason for that was, to make sure, the new driver is careful and responsible with handling the car. So, my first pick up was at a very busy shopping mall, in a suburb of Chicago. I had a hard time to locate the person, because there were so many point to look for him. But finally I found him, he was a business man and wanted to go to the airport. I know today, I did not take the shortest route, because I was not too familiar with the new system of streets. But I got him there and he was very nice and once we had figured out the credit card swipe, he even gave me a tip and I wished him a good flight.

The first few weeks, I had to concentrate very hard on everything I did. But then, became familiar with a lot of things and felt a happy feeling in me. Now I really had the chance to meet all kinds of people and it was fun.

From big shots of the Motorola company, down to the ordinary people, that came back from a visit to one of their family members. Most of the people were friendly and I had many nice conversations with them and almost everybody was generous with the tip.

A few months had gone by and I was still driving a regular car, when one day, when I picked up a car for the day, finally I got a stretch. It was an older Cadillac and had some bad spots on the inside. I was so thrilled, that the first thing I did, I got this car to the car wash and after it was clean on the outside, I took off my jacked and started to clean the entire inside. After about one hour, I was satisfied with what I did and sat behind the wheel, looking full of pride and put a smile on my face.

The next call I got, was to pick up a woman and her daughter. Once I got them in the car, I felt like I was transporting royalty to their castle. The castle was the airport and when we got there, I looked around to make sure a lot of other drivers did see me.

In the meantime I built up a good reputation and a good relationship with our dispatchers. After a few more weeks, they let me drive a fairly new stretch. But now, I was used to the way we did business and became relaxed. From then on I was always curious, who my next party was. To expand my driving horizon, I attended a special driving seminar in Chicago, to get a permit to drive in the big city. After that I got a special car with special license plate. However a few months later, I went back into a suburban car, because I could make more money

Every Sunday morning, when I had my days off, my brother and his girl friend went to a certain restaurant for brunch, to meet us. Both of them always were very interested to hear what I had to tell them about the past week. We always laughed and had a really good time, talking about other people. Especially amusing were the once, when I had a private female party on Saturday nights, that wanted to go and bar hop. I was chartered and had to stand by them at any time. It was always a very nice experience, when I had to car full of women, bar hopping. Many times they were together to meet their husbands later. Many of these women had a serious job during the week and tried to relax on the weekend. Sometimes I had them for many hours and of course, they got more tipsy by the minute. After many times, they involved me in a conversation and I felt real good about my job. When I finally unloaded them on their last stop to meet their husbands, all of the sudden my car was so empty. It was different with guys, they were always boisterous and used profanities. Well, I was friendly with them, but was relieved after my car was empty.

On many occasions I was a witness of very serious conversations, between VIPs' that mostly had to solve problems within their company. Many times when we got to their company, they asked me to stay a little longer until their conversation came to an end. Of course I didn't want to listen in, but the inside of my car was all open and nobody, asked me to close the divider. So, I learned a lot of things, that I didn't know about. Especially interesting were the conversations between Bankers.

So, our lives were normal and we had no problems, except that I had to work odd hours, sometimes through the whole night. My wife had started a job at a local news paper and was also working the late shift. We adjusted our lives to the circumstances and we were quite happy

I was still working there after three years and new everything about my job. Many times, when I parked at the special parking lot at the airport and had some time to kill, I followed the starting airplanes, many of them destined for foreign countries. I got a little soft, by remembering my time, when I had to use a lot of them, and I thought, with my experience in sales, there should be a company, that needed somebody like me. I don't know what happened, on the next day, I got a call from my young friend in Germany. After we said a friendly hello, he told me, that he and his boss had been to a trade show, where among other American companies, he discovered one, that had a very interesting product on display. It was special paint, that in Germany nobody was familiar with and his boss showed great interest in it. The reason he called me was to asked me to find out more about that company. They were trying to talk to the people at the booth, but nobody spoke the German language. He gave their name and phone number and I told him, I would take care of that.

The next day I made a call to them and was lucky to speak to the sales manager. I introduced myself and told him, that I had a good lead from the last show they had in Germany. When he told me, that he would be happy to send me some info's to extend to the people in Germany, I asked him, if he didn't have somebody to represent him at the European market that spoke German. That was very important, because Germany is the industrial heart of Europe. Among all the languages being spoken in Europe, you need to speak either

German or English. When he said "No" I asked him if he would be interested to hire one. His answer was, that they were actually looking for a export manager. When I asked him if I would have a chance, he told me to send in my papers so they could take a look at them. Wow, I felt that that was a great chance for me. Because as I found out, this company was a family enterprise, established thirty years ago and the paint that they were selling was leading the national market for many years.

Being very cautiously optimistic and tried not show everybody my excitement, I sat down and wrote my resume the old fashion way. The way I had learned it back in the old country. A little later, when I spoke to my youngest daughter about that, she, being an active "Headhunter" and used to very fancy resumes, started smiling and wished me good luck with it.

A few weeks went by, when one day the phone rang and the sales manager was on the phone, he told me that he got my papers and his boss and himself would be interested to talk to me at the upcoming hardware show in Chicago.

CHAPTER 15

· ·

Disappointment!

He told me to meet him at certain place just outside of the show building on a Sunday morning. Stifling my enthusiasm to a point that it hurt. That Sunday I got there early enough to make sure, I found the right spot, that he pointed out to me in our phone call. When I got there, I noticed very soon, that a couple of things were not exactly right. The revolving doors he talked about were not on the upper floor, but at the main entrance on the lower one. So, thinking that the revolving doors were the most important to follow, I waited almost an hour and nobody showed up.

I could feel my disappointment creeping up on me, but I was not willing to give up that easy. After on other thirty minute or so, I went up to the main show office and asked them for the booth number of this company. They looked it up and told me where it was located. Since I didn't have a pass to get into the hall, they issued me a temporary one.

It took me a little time to find the area where they had their booth. When I finally saw it, I slowed down and stood at a little distance to see what was going on in there. I noticed a few people, who seemed to be with that company. It was still early and there were no visiting people in sight. I notice a very tall man with white hair, who paced along the outside of the booth. I waited a few more minutes and started to move toward that place. I waited until I had that tall man right in front of me. I looked at him and said a friendly: "Hi." He looked at me and said the same thing. When he asked me, how he could help me, I introduced myself. After he heard my name, he pointed to me and said: "Your are the man, we are waiting for. Our sale manager is roaming around the building and is looking for you." After I explained to him what was wrong, he invited me to sit down. At the same time, here came the sales manager.

The tall man, which had introduce himself to me as the owner and president of the company, turned to him, pointing at me, and told him with a determined voice that I was sitting here and was waiting for him.

When I cleared that misunderstanding about the revolving doors, we all sat down and started a Q an A session. We talked about general things like where I was from and what kind of experience I had. I explained to them just enough, to get interested and was careful not to over talk myself. After they had answered all of my questions, I waited for them to come to an end of this session. It didn't take too long and they thanked me for joining them and we shook hands and said bye. Before I left, I asked them what the time line was for an answer, I was told approximately two weeks, because they had several other people on their list. I turned around, stepped into the booth again on the other end, where the other people were standing and told them my name and asked them, if they could explain the functioning of their products. They were willing to do that and after a few minutes, I was doing it. I liked what I saw and said bye to them.

Now, coming home and telling all of that to my wife, a very hard time started to begin. I was still driving my limo, but was only thinking about that meeting. Time had gone by and my hope to get that job was dwindling, when on a Monday morning the phone rang and the sales manager was on the line and told me, that the president wanted to see me in his office and talk to me some more. Besides me, he told me, that they had someone else coming in for a closer look. He gave me a choice, to come over on one of two days, for a meeting with the two of us. When I asked him what days that were, he said either Monday or Tuesday of next week. I decided to make it on Tuesday, to give the president the chance to focus more on me. It was a good decision. As the sales manager told me later, that the guy that was there before me, and spoke six languages was, as he said it: "Too slick." We set a date and when I got to their airport the sales manager was waiting for me.

Their office was located inside of a very old building, that had served its purpose from the first day of manufacturing their first pot of paint.

At this meeting the president went into more details and was constantly reading my old fashion resume. After about two hours, right before lunch, we were done and after I got paid for my expenses, the sales manager invited me to go to eat with him. During lunch, I noticed he was not very talkative. But the hour went by and he offered me to take me to the airport. He did and I was on time back in Chicago.

This time, it didn't take too long, when after two days suddenly in the morning the phone rang again and the CFO of the corporation was asking me, after he told me my pay schedule, if I would except the position as a export manager for the company. I had to control myself and said with a calm voice: "Yes, of course."

That seemed the end of my wife's and my insecure living, This company was a solid "Nest" as I called it. I knew, this was the opportunity I had waited for my whole life. A dream came true. We hugged each other for a long time and I thanked her for being there for me all the time.

To start my job officially, they were waiting for me the following Tuesday. After a very friendly reception, the sales manager asked me to follow him and introduced me to a lot of important people. This took a few hours and ended up right before lunch. The president came and asked me to go to eat with him. As I said before, He was a very tall man and I had to keep a little distance between him and me, not to strain my neck too much to look up to him. He took his very new Cadillac and drove me to a famous restaurant in down town Scranton.

When we sat down, surrounded by his peers, he told them about me and made me say some things in German. I felt a little funny, but it was o.k. with me, because obviously he felt good about it. I had a very good feeling about him and that feeling stayed with me all the years I represented him and his company. They told me, that, because I lived very close to the O'Hara airport in Chicago, I could work out of my home office.

After I went through a information training of one week, I now was the official export manager. The export business so far was pitiful. In all their years they accumulated only a small fraction of the total sales of the company. They had set up a couple of dealers in two different countries, which had never increased their sales of their products. My first job was, to go through a lot of years of old business letters, that were not followed up.

My last day, I spent at the office, I went to the sales manager to tell him, that we needed a special price list for export. I was told, to hold back on that and just to learn their products. I was very surprised to hear that, because over the years, I had learned that any company, that exported their products, had higher prices listed in their export list.

When I came home and my wife and I went out for a fancy dinner that night, we were the happiest couple on this earth.

In preparation for my first trade show in Germany, I had a hard time to find any paper work that could help me in Europe. So, what I did, I translated a lot of flyers that I had, printed in English into German. I sent a copy of each to our main office and after a while, I got the first compliment on my work I had done so far.

After a few weeks I got the message, that before we go the show in Germany, the president and the sales manager, wanted to go to England and see some possible clients. This trip included me and they told me all about the contacts they had made over the years, with foreign companies. As the export manager, my boss was now eager to let me meet some of them.

I was advised to stay at a certain hotel in down town London. When I got the airport very early in the morning, I took a typical London cab, and enjoyed the ride. When we drove through down town, a very funny feeling came over me. All of the sudden, I was aware, that this city was bombed by the Germans very heavily. Looking at these high rise buildings next to me, I couldn't imagine, what those poor people had to go through. I myself had experienced some bomb attacks, initiated by the allied troops, nearby in our city. But that was all flat land and everybody had a chance to go into a shelter outside of the city.

When I got to the hotel, it was around noon. As I found out later, this was the most expensive place in London. First difference, I noticed, when I got into the foyer was, there was no reception desk. After looking a bit around I saw a table lined up next to the door of an adjacent room and occupied by a very expensive clad man. I walked over to him and asked him, where I could check in. He told me, that I was at the right room. Then he shoved a book over to me and asked me to fill in the empty spaces.

I did that and he gave me not only a cold shoulder, but also a key for a room. Later on, I found out, that the cold shoulder was because of my American address. Obviously an common American was not exactly what they represented. What he didn't know was, that I was proud to work for man, that had earned my trust and was American.

Once I found my room I had to figure out how to open the door. When I finally found the secret how to open it, it was a combination of numbers and a certain position in which you heard a click, and the door opened. When I entered the room, I was very surprised of the size.

It was very small and I had a problem to get my suitcase to the other side. Once I had it placed, I was looking for a TV. At first glance, I couldn't find it. But not believing that there was no TV in the room, I discovered it. Because of the room was so small, they had mounted it way high, close to the sealing. That way you couldn't bump into it with your head. Since it was the month on March, the weather outside was not very inviting and therefore, the inside of the room was like an enemy. It was cold and wet and therefore very uncomfortable.

The next morning, I took a closer look at the bathroom and noticed, that the metal frame, that was mounted on top of the tub and followed its curves, held a very colorful heavy glass window. I also noticed at the end of the tub, a couple of red buttons sticking out of the wall. I wondered what they were for. Then I noticed, that the bottom of the glass was mounted about two inches higher than the upper end of the tub.

CHAPTER 16

. . . .

Learning again!

It came as it had to come, when I was taking my shower, most of the water drained between the glass and the tub, which created a big lake of water outside of the tub on the floor. I also noticed, that the bottom of the tub was rounded upwards to both sides. That gave you a very hard time to keep your balance, because you had to put your feet in front of each other. Now I knew, what these red buttons were for. After a fall you could use them to get help.

When I was finally finished with everything, I went down to get my breakfast. So, the next thing I did, was locating a table. The coffee that was served was very strong and had no coffee taste left. Since I had some hotel guests, most of them Arabs, sitting around me, I pretended that coffee was exactly what I wanted.

When I was done with my breakfast, I saw our president and our sales manager accompanied by two women. When they noticed me, the gestured me to come over to their table. When I got there, I was introduced to the women as their wives. I got a warm hello from both. However, I noticed, the elderly woman was moving very slowly and after starting a conversation with them, I also noticed a slur in her speaking. Than I was told, that this lady was the wife of our president and had suffered a heavy stroke a few years back. By this time, and after many years of therapy, at least she was able to hold a slow conversation. The other woman, was introduced to me as our Sales managers wife. That morning, my president asked me to call him by his first name, which was Mac.

Since he was so very tall, he was called by everyone "Big Mac."

This breakfast took longer than usual. When we were done, our sales manager went out to get train tickets to a town about one hour away from London, toward Liverpool. The two women said bye and went to down town to see the stores. The younger woman was to accompany Macs wife, to make sure, she was o.k.

From the train, I noticed, that the suburbs of London were not very pretty to look at. It looked to me, as if they hadn't seen maintenance for many years. I was a little disappointed to see that. Once we got into the country, everything looked a lot better. The sun was shining and after an hour or so, we arrived at a very small town. Besides the train station, we couldn't see any other buildings. Looking around, Big Mac said: "We'll find something." and started walking in a certain direction. My sales manager and I looked at each other, shrug our shoulders and follow him. After we went by a couple of hills, we noticed a big factory building, which contained several smaller businesses. Among those was the one we were looking for.

My respect for my boss, grew bigger. How did he know the location of this building. But since he was of Irish descent, he probably had a sixth sense for that. Since we had some time to kill, Mac lead us into a old fashion Irish pub, which was located inside of that big building. He felt like home in no time and had a big conversation with some of their guests. We all enjoyed it very much.

Once we found the company we had an appointment with, we were received in a nice manner. My first problem I had, was with their language. I had never been in the UK and it took me some time, to get acquainted with it.

Our meeting partner of this company was a younger man, with a typical English demeanor. Since we were three people, I took a seat more in the back and gave the sales manager and the president the chance to talk directly to that man., after all, I was there to mostly listen to what they had to say.

After our sales manager had done a demonstration of a couple of our products, the young man told us, that he was willing to do something with our products, but he had to clear it with his boss first. But the way he said it, made me think, that he was not serious about it, and I was right. Of all the next three visits in several towns in England, we never got an order. This was my first lesson I learned about the mentality of the English. Having learned about that, a year later I was able to set up a dealer on the outskirts of London.

Coming back home, I prepared myself for the upcoming show in Germany. My company had rented a space at the show together with the American Hardware Association. This was a very expensive matter. The advantages we had was, that in case we needed a translator, there was one available at any time. We also had free access to a coffee shop, set up next to our space. Our booth was very small und could hold only three people at one time. In spite of this disadvantage, we had a lot of interested people to stop at our booth and wanted to hear and see what we had to offer.

Now, the German show was not only important for us to get customers in Germany, but it was more important, because it was visited by many people from foreign countries, especially from eastern Europe, that had emerged after the Sowjet Union had collapsed. We heard languages, that were not known to us and even all the languages our translators spoke, were not enough to help us. So, we had to make clear to these people what we had to offer, with our arms and hands. However, we never took an order from one of them, because there was no way to collect their moneys. However at the first show in Germany for me, I got several serious leads in Western Europe.

When we got home, I sent out emails and info's to all the people, that had shown interest at the show and left their business cards. Of all the info packages I sent out, I got only a few answers back, but never got an order. All that company money I spent on sending these packages around the world, was in my opinion wasted. Coming back to my mind, were all the people I saw at the shows, with bags full of information of kinds of products. I often wondered, if all this really would be read by them. So, at the future shows I attended, I figured out right a way from the beginning of a sales conversation with a visitor at our booth, how serious he or she sounded. After they had their saying, I begun to asked them special questions and demonstrated our products in a way, the customer had to get involved with and on their reaction, I could pretty much tell, if their interest was real or pretend. When I was done with them and they asked me to send them more info, I asked them, if it would be o.k. if I gave them a single flyer with my business card stapled to and after they had another talk or two, back home at their office, to make sure they still were interested. Than to send me an email and I would be happy to sent them our info package. They all agreed with that and at the same time, I improved the quality of my beginning relationship with them. I knew, they kept their word and I kept mine.

At one of our shows in Germany, we still had that little space, I had a visitor from France. I knew by this time, that the French people were very negligent to speak another language, but so far we always were able to get through to them. My German helped out many times. This man however, did not meet us half way to communicate with him, when at one point I needed one of our translators. When she came over she spoke to the French man and asked him, how she could help. After back and forth between French and German, there was a word in English, that had like many other English words, more than on meaning. When I tried to explain the second meaning, which referred to our paint, neither the French man nor the translator knew to explain it. When finally the French man got very nervous, turned around and walked away. After that, and for the future, I didn't want a translator anymore.

After the second show in Germany, we still had that small booth, I approached my boss, to asked him, if it would be o.k. with him, if I would get some info to get our own space and our own display, away from the American section. He said yes and got good news, a much bigger space was available for a lot of less money. So, I designed my own booth and the next year, we had a beautiful looking display. By now, we were visited by many f our competitors and by listening to them, I knew, we were at the right place.

CHAPTER 17

· ·

Building up business!

In spite of the fact, that the Germans were on top of the chemical ladder, we had something here, that they had not.

In the meantime, I had followed up some of the leads from the last show. The first new customer from oversees, was a company from Poland. After some emails I was visited from two young men here in the US. We met at a hotel near a big shopping mall, and for the next two hours we were busy to listen to each other. When they left, I knew I had an order coming.

I was right, a couple of weeks later, I got an order for a half container full of our products. After we took care of the financial situation in this case like any other case, the first orders had to be paid in advanced, until we saw the natural growing of their business. That meant, that they had to go to their local shows and their orders had to be increased. Of course, we supported them at their shows, by paying half of their floor space and a visit by me.

Within that year, I set up more dealers in two more countries. Most of these businesses were set up new, others had already a retail store and added our products to theirs. In the meantime, we had our local shows and we had more and more people wanted to talk to us repeatedly.

One of the countries was the Philippines. The contact we made, was at the Chicago Hardware show. This visitor was a young Chinese, who was very interested to see what we had to offer. After a while he and I got involved in a very serious talk and at the end of our talk, he gave me the guarantee, to become a partner of my company. After a little while I received as email, and a big order. Immediately he ordered a full container. When I asked him why such a big order, since he had not a big knowledge, he said that he had known about our product a long time ago, because a few years ago he was living for more than five years in a city in Texas.

We shipped everything over to him and when his next show in Manila came up, I went there to help him. The show was a huge success and after meeting his father and his wife as well as his brother and sister, we had a great time together. I used my extra time to go with my new partner and follow up leads we had from the show. The weather over there is mostly rain and high humidity. The street traffic was awful and always bumper to bumper. When at one point we had to stop again and the rain was still coming down, we noticed a whole bunch of kids, that were selling things to the drivers, bending over the hood and started licking the rain from it. When I turned to my side, of the car, I saw a beautiful little face of a girl. She was dressed like a little doll and held something in her little hand. When I saw her eyes, I was spell bound and was not able to take my eyes off of her.

She kept staring at me. Unfortunately, before I was able to take some money out of my pocket, the driver moved the car forward again and I lost her. I tried to locate her again, but was not able to do that. When my partner saw my sad face, he told me, that I shouldn't be sad, because the girl had to give the money to a hustler anyways. That didn't make me feel any better, because I wanted to give that girl money, not because of the hustler, but because of me. I still can see her eyes and that still makes me sad.

The whole situation in the Philippines looked helpless. The vast majority of the population lives under the poverty line and I wished, I could do something big over there, especially for the young girls.

At one point, I thought it would be a good idea, to learn another language. The thought that came up was, Mexican. Since I had learned, that the vast majority of people on this earth spoke that language. So, I went out and got a tape, telling me how easy it was to speak that language. Since I had the experience with that situation when I came to the States, I had no reservations and started listening to that tape all day long. Yes, they were right, to learn that language was relatively easy. So, the next show we had in Europe, I was prepared to face any body that only spoke Spanish.

The days of the next show in Germany had arrived. We had now a much bigger and much nicer place to show for. I knew we had to do that, because in Europe, Germany was the industrial leader and Europe followed that lead. Very important for a foreign company was, to show their faces. The people wanted to know, where you came from and how stable was your company. Of course we were looking for wholesalers in any country and they had to know, that you were there when they needed you. Of course we had a very solid back ground and were listed the seventh richest family company in the US. Now it was my duty to make them trust me and my company.

One thing I never did was, to push the visitors. I left it completely up to them, to make up their minds. When I got to the point in a conversation were the visitors among each other, were discussing the possibilities, to adopt our products, I took a step back and let them come up with a plan. Most of the time, these VIP's of a company made up their minds right there and referred me to another person in charge of import at their company.

So, I was on my way up and spent a lot of time to follow these leads within any country in Europe, before I went back home. At these times, I made a lot of friends and many of these people are still in my phonebook today.

In the following year, I set up six new countries, including Sweden with all the Scandinavian neighbors. All the shows in their respected countries were successful and made their owners very happy.

The one country I heard about a lot, was China. I had heard controversial stories about it, and the next time, we had our annual meeting with the DIY World Council, out of Indianapolis, at one of the islands in the Caribbean Sea, I wanted to know more. After our morning sessions, we had a chance to select one of the tables, that were discussing business in different countries. I selected the Chinese table. The head of the table was young man of Chinese descent and after we were introduced to him, the first thing he said was: "Don't do business in China!"

After we all settled down, we asked for an explanation. He begun to explain, that the Chinese people had a hard time to trust anybody out side of their family and they always had in mind to copy anything that came from there. One big example of that was sitting next to us. When they were introduced to us, one of the young men, who was a co-owner of their company, started to tell us, what happened to them.

They were manufacturing high quality, designer faucets. After many years of having success, they met a Chinese business man at a show, they attended. After a few hours of negotiating they came to a deal. The Chinese company ordered a full load of their products. After that was paid for, it was shipped and everybody seemed happy, with the thought, to be able to open the Chinese market.

After four months, they hadn't heard anything from the new customers, and both of the boys went over to China to see, if the Chinese would need any help. How surprised they were, to see in stores, what they thought to be their products. After closer inspection, they noticed that these faucets were duplicated. They bought two of them and took them home, to get the attention of the American Trade Commission, but they told them, that nothing could be done except to go with an international lawyer group, which not only was very expensive, but as the lawyer told them a little later, it would be impossible to get through to the courts in China. The two owners dropped that case and made sure, that no Chinese would ever get a hand on their products again.

Yeah, I had heard these stories many times, that that had happened to the American products, that were distributed in China. Except for some American companies. I found out through my company, that those products made by big manufactures here in the States only had a chance to do business in China, because they had the meaning to go after them, and had the back up from the American Trade Commission.

CHAPTER 18

. . . .

Preparing for the Chinese!

So, a couple of years went by, when at one day, at a show in Chicago, I saw a Chinese woman coming in our booth. She was of solid stature and when I approached her, she answered me in very good English. So, with all the warning signals that I saw in front of my eyes, I saw her coming a little closer to our display. She really begun to take a closer look at it. For some minutes neither of us said anything. Finally, she begun to asked me some questions.

Immediately I noticed that the question she asked, contained some chemical knowledge. Because we were told by our chemists, that we only could answer general questions. I told her, that I didn't know the answers for these question and that I had to go to our lab to get them. When I asked her, if it would be possible to meet her after the show, so I could spend more time with her, she said yes and told me her address. In fact her location was located in one of the Chicagoan suburbs. Since I could see, that she was very serious in this matter, I though, I could give it a chance. We set a date and met at my office at my house.

When she came in time one afternoon, I had prepared myself for her and had talked to my chemists about this meeting. He advised me what I could tell her. We had a very lively conversation and I was careful not to say anything wrong.

After a few weeks, I got a call from her, asking me, if she could talk to one of our chemists. When I asked her if she would understand everything that had to be said about the chemicals of our product, she told me, that she herself was a chemist by trade. Our meeting ended with mixed feelings. I informed my lab and was interested to see, what was coming out of all this. In the future, she tried to talk a few more times with our lab people, but they did not take any more calls from her.

When after a few more weeks, she called me again and ask me if she could order some samples to try them on her mother's house, which had a big problem with water leakage on the inside. Without letting my company know, I sent her a can of our product by airmail.

Here again, weeks went by and I didn't even think about her any more, when she gave me a call and told me, that she just had come back from China. She asked me for a meeting and we settled for the next day at lunch. When we met at a restaurant, she was very excited to tell me, that they had applied our paint to their inside wall of her mother's apartment, and when the next rain came, it did not penetrate the walls. Everybody was very happy about that and that convinced her to trust us.

After I talked to our lab people again and told them that she was willing to give us an order, they told me, that that was o.k., because even if they tried to copy our product, it would not be possible, because there was a part of the mixture, that could not be indentified under a microscope. So, I was all set for her to give me a order. I didn't count on too much, but how big was my surprise when she ordered a whole container load.

After the order was properly taken care of and it was shipped, she called me in for a meeting with an member of her company. That meeting was two days after her phone call and the place was at a hotel, not too far from where she lived. I was waiting only a few minutes, when I saw her, accompanied by an elderly Gentleman, that turned out to be the top manager of her company. He was introduced to me as the former CEO of the biggest electro manufacturer in the world, located in Schaumburg, Il. He was now retired and had started a export company, not only for electronics, but also for any materials that could be suited for the Chinese market. After we ordered lunch, he congratulated me for being able to start a business relationship with his Chinese partner. He asked me all kinds of questions about my past with her. I told him about the difficulties we had and that at one point, we were thinking of not doing business with her. After he had listened to me for an hour or so, he looked at me got up and asked me if he could hug me. I was shocked not only because I had an offer to hug a very big man, but mostly because that was completely out of order. He noticed my strange look on my face, started to smile and said: "It's o.k. but I have never met a salesman, that had the guts to honestly tell the truth. and had the courage to take on the Chinese market."

Of course, that was a big lesson in my life as a salesman, especially when it came from a high ranking individual as this man was.

It didn't take too long before I got the message from her, that they applied for an space at the upcoming show in Shanghai. Negotiations went back and forth and at one point we agreed on a plan and my travel plan was set for about two days before the show started.

This was a good opportunity to take my wife with me and I did. After a very long flight, crossing the international date line, we arrived in Shanghai around noon time. She was there with an younger man and took us to our hotel. This trip took more than one and a half hour. When we finally got there, we saw a very huge very modern building. Even though we were very tired, but noticed on the way to the hotel, how modern everything looked. The vision of China we had all these years, was kind of dreary, but we had to learn a lot.

The first night, before we went to go to sleep, she had arranged a private party, with some Chinese people and herself. We had the whole room for our self's and as the guests of honor, I had to sit on her right and my wife on her left side. After everybody had arrived, she said something in her language to all the other guests, that made them look at us all the time. When she was done with her speech, she then gave the order to serve the dinner. Here we learned a lot more. The big round table had a elevated smaller also round plate mounted in the center of the table. When the servers came with the food, they placed everything on that plate and turned it slowly, so the food items could pass every guest, who was then privileged, to take from that plate anything they wished. Once that plate was fully loaded and had gone by me and my wife a few times, we had a hard time to decide what we would like. That was very hard to determine, because we had no idea what we were looking at. Nothing looked like we had eaten before in our lives. My wife kept looking at me, to see what kind of food I would go for. I looked at her and shrug my shoulders. When everybody else had loaded their plates, we were still looking for the right thing.

When our hostess noticed our dilemma, she turned to us and asked if she could help us to find something to eat for us. Since she was very familiar with the life and the food in the US, after all she had become American citizen just a few months ago, she than pointed out some foods, that we could eat. I followed her advice and so did my wife. After we were all done, we had eaten only a fraction of what the other people ate. I apologized for that, but of course she understood.

The next morning, we were ready to go to the show, when she got a call from the immigration office, to come to them and explained a shipment of show displays coming from our office in the US.

When we got there we entered a old wooden building and stepped into a very funny smelling office. Later I found out, that the smell came from the old wood and uniforms. The man in charge was of little stature and it looked like, his uniform was much too big for him. He looked clean, but whenever he moved his head to the left or right, his military cap did not follow this movement and stayed straight. That was a humoristic picture and I had a hard time to stifle my amusement.

The problem was, that our items were shipped on a wooden pallet, which was not allowed by the Chinese government. The reason for that was, to prevent the importation of bugs. This incident lead to a big problem and it took all of us, the whole day to get this resolved. In the meantime, all the customers to this office were looking at us. The rest of the office crew was made up of young girls. My partner had to talk a lot and finally, the top guy made a decision and freed our shipment.

CHAPTER 19

· ·

The future?

When that was done, I looked at the crew and thanked them for their efforts, when all the girls came toward me and said in perfect English, how pleased they were, to have met us. When we walked out, everybody had a smile on their face. This was again a valuable experience for me. She took us to our hotel and told us, that she could not pick us up the next morning and we were supposed to take a cab. That morning, after we walked out of the room, we were looking for a breakfast room, when we were told, that here was more than one room to eat in the morning. We selected the one that was located in the "Western" section.

The food that was offered, was to our liking.

Once we were done, we went to the reception desk and called for one of the cabs, that were waiting for customers in front of the building. We told the concierge to make sure, that the cab driver could understand English. He immediately nodded his head and waved to the first cab. When it stopped at the main door, the driver came and got our little luggage and asked us in Chinese something. When we said something in English, he said "Yes" and we went with him. I explained the goal and he got us there in about fifteen minutes. The taxi meter showed a amount in Chinese and when I converted it into dollars, it was very low price. Seeing our partner at the booth, she said, that the cab fares in China were cheap.

Once we opened the show, we attracted a lot of construction people, who had never seen anything like our product. The day went by fast and the following night, after my wife and I had a short conversation about China so far, we were falling asleep very shortly.

The coming day went just about the same. The next morning, when we took a cab again, I noticed pretty soon, that the driver was not familiar with the route to our show. He stopped a few times to asked some people how to get there. When he stopped to ask a policeman and didn't get an answer, I told him to go back to the hotel. He looked at me with a blank face and I found out, that he did not speak any English. Looking at my wife, I remembered, when we checked in, the hotel gave us a welcome card with their name and address in both languages. I showed it to the driver and he understood and took us back to the hotel. When we arrived there, I looked at the meter and reached over to him, to give him the money. He looked at me and pushed my hand back and shook his head, by pointing at the meter. I knew what he meant, but insisted to take the money, because I was happy to see, that the driver knew it was his fault and wouldn't want to be paid for. I knew, that the average Chinese did not make a lot of money, so, I insisted and with a happy face he finally excepted it. We than called another cab and made sure from now on, that all the cabs we used in the future, had a driver that spoke at least a little English.

When the show was over and we had seen and experienced a lot of new things, we saw China in a different light. We visited shopping malls and were surprised to see the personal, all tall, great looking women, being very friendly. The stores had a huge selection of very modern products of any kind. We were actually spell bounded to see more and more of surprises that day and all the other days following.

Every night when we came back to our hotel we were recognized as the "Westerners." and automatically guided to our special dinner table.

The following morning, my partner called us and asked us, if we were o.k. to fly the a town, not too far away from Shanghai and were ready to meet the mayor of this huge city. We were already used to the sizes of towns and cities and the town we were supposed to go was also of a gigantic size, located at the south China sea. When we got there, they had booked a room at a fife star hotel in the center of town. We got there in the middle of the afternoon and had some time to take a walk around the hotel. It was a very lovely town, with parks and streets designed to please the people. It had a very mild climate and Edy and I had some time to sit at a bench with a view of the sea. We needed that and when we returned to the hotel, we were different people.

We went back to our rooms and were called back into the present, by a call. We were told, that our partner had arranged a meeting with the mayor at eight o'clock. When we got close to that time, we were guided to a special dining room at the second floor. This room was of generous size with a long flat cocktail table, surrounded by many majestic looking chairs. Flowers were distributed all over.

We were waiting a few minutes and when nobody showed up, I went outside of the room, to see, if there was any movement toward us. When I stopped at the banister, I could look down to the lobby. As everything else, it was also of very large size. After a few seconds I noticed our partner walking toward the main door and half way there, the door opened and a bunch of men came through. Lead by a tall man who went over to her and greeted her very friendly. They had a small talk and the men went over to see the hotel manager. In the meantime, my partner came up to us and told us about the arrival of the mayor. We confirmed it, when she asked me, if had nothing better to wear, she pointed at my casual jacket and notice, that I was not wearing a tie. I told her, that I was not prepared for this and to tell the mayor, that I was very sorry about that.

After a while, she came back to us and asked us to sit in one of the chairs. We did and only a while later, here comes the mayor, followed by all of his eight men. When I took a closer look at the mayor, I noticed, he was not wearing a jacket or a tie. Later on I was told that he took them off, to accommodate my appearance. That gave me a good feeling. Than we were introduced to all of them and were told, that the men were all technical support for the mayor and couldn't speak English except for one of his escorts, his name was Payphone, who had lived in San Francisco for a few years, and spoke very good English and told me, that he would translate my conversation with the mayor. They also brought a photographer to take pictures of our meeting. The mayor and I were guided to the end of the table, where two chairs were waiting for us. Before we could sit down, we had to look into the camera and with a hand shake and a smile.

The mayor and I had a short conversation, and I praised what we had seen in his country. I promised him to go back to the American people and tell them about what we had seen and experienced. He was very happy to hear that and wished me and my wife a long and happy life.

After he had left, his escort stayed and invited us to a dinner. Of course we couldn't say no and waited for thing to come. Payphone translated the conversations as good as he could, because all of them wanted to talk to us.

After the food was served and we started drinking a few glasses of wine, we noticed, that all of the men all of the sudden, spoke almost fluently English. A day later, when we were driven around in the city in a city car, driven by an government employee, we were talking about the men that spoke suddenly English. We were told, that it took some time for them to get a good feeling about us. But once they noticed we were worth it, they opened up and we had a great time.

The following days, we spent our time back in Shanghai and were nicely surprised how the Chinese people reacted to us and we hoped, that all the smiles we saw, came from their hearts and not only from their faces.

After we were done with everything we had to do, we were ready to go back home. So, we took a taxi from the hotel to the airport and here again, I was very surprised how low the fare was. When we left the cab, I noticed a new construction, that looked like they were building some kind of a rail, going into the big city. Later I found out, that I was right. This was the beginning of the from Germany imported magnet train. When we got back to the US, we had to change our thinking. For the next few days Edy and I were just talking about the trip and looked at the pictures we had taken. One incidence we clearly recalled with humor was, when we were driving to the airport, we used a very wide road with four lanes on either side.

Divided by a beautiful line of flowers, we noticed one of the people on a bike totally packed with empty wooden baskets to a point, that you couldn't see the man. This guy obviously had lost a few of his baskets and what he did, he parked his bike in the middle of the road and went after his lost baskets. Since this road was very wide and not being used by too many cars, which were going a very high speed and thus creating a very dangerous situation. The man was lucky not to be hit by one of them. Once he had mounted all of his lost baskets on his bike again, he then proceeded on his route, in the middle of the road.

In the following years, I went on to display our products on as many shows I could get. On one of those, I got a visitor from the Island of Cypress.

They were a young couple and had just taken over the established business, that his father had founded many years ago. When he saw our display, he got very excited and after a good demonstration of our product, he asked me, if it would be possible for me to come to his island and perform a display show, as we had here right now. After I explained the conditions for that, he agreed with all of them and we set a preliminary date. Not long after that, I got an email from him in which suggested a date, four weeks later.

CHAPTER 20

· ·

Learning history!

I confirmed it and we sent out a appropriate order and made sure, we had some of our display fixtures included.

When I got there, I met all of his coworkers and was introduced to a very large oil painting, showing his father. Since the island was not very large to accompany big industries, all the businesses were located near the Mediterranean sea. We had two more days to go for the show, to set it up. His store was located on the bottom of a fairly new building. The second floor served as his main office and a large empty room, that could be used for many purposes. This room was now set up for our show. In the meantime I was told, that his company had done a lot of advertising through TV, papers and radio. So, they expected approximately 100 people to com. The room was set up in a manner, that on one side we held our show, the other side was set up with tables and offered dinner for the guests.

So, when the time arrived, the first visitors came up the elevator and were directed to the dinner side. I noticed everybody was very nicely dressed and in no time we had our room full of people. After an hour or so, the announcement was made, that the demonstration was now beginning. When everybody was sitting, we counted 98 people, one TV station, two newspapers and two radio stations. Since a lot of people didn't speak English, we had arranged, that the sister of the owner, who had learned to speak the language at a collage, as the translator into Greek. The whole session was over after three hours. Everybody was very interested and I had to answer a lot of questions. The real success we saw the next day, when many of the participants of the show, came and bought almost everything we had on display.

For my visits to a foreign country, I always took an extra two days off, to learns more about the people and the land. Cypress was partially occupied by the Turkish. So, the Island was kind of split between the Greeks and them. The bigger part belonged to the Greeks and gave me a chance to visit many villages and the greater part of the Island. Since Cypress is a very historical place, I had a chance to see the birth place of Aphrodite's, which is known today as a goddess of the Greek Mythology.

Time went by and my job kept me busy as a liaison between my customers and my company. When the orders came in, I had to clear them up to make sure, that our office people could process them efficiently. Ever since, the export sale was climbing, sometimes things didn't go perfectly and we had to make some changes in our international rules and regulations. Once we were settled with it, things went a lot smoother and we were one big happy family. The next show in Germany, we still had our nice big booth, we met a woman who had a business at the island of Mauritius.

Located in the Indian Ocean, on the east coast of Africa, across Madagascar. She told me, that she had seen us at one of the previous shows, but didn't have the chance to talk to one of us. When she knew all about our products, she agreed to become our dealer at her island. When I told her the conditions we required to become one, she agreed with them and we set a date for me to come to her place at the time, when they had a show at the island.

A few months went by when she gave me a message, That the material had arrived and was all ready for the show, which followed a couple of weeks later. I made my preparations and after a very long flight, across Europe and the Mediterranean sea, Africa and Madagascar, I got there around noon. She and her assistant were waiting for me at the air port. What I had heard about this island, were nothing but praises. A few times it was called paradise or heaven. I was kind of disappointed, when the air plane came closer the ground, the only thing I saw, were very big fields of something.

When we got into the car, I was looking forward to get into a bed, no matter where it was. When we started driving, not long, we were right into one of these fields. When I took a closer look, I thought I was looking at bamboo, about ten feet high. When I asked the people what this is, I was told, the island was a major producer of sugarcane. So, the next one hour we drove through these fields, when we finally got to a hotel, outside of the city of Port Louis. This was a Sheraton hotel, located directly next to the sea. It was huge property and looked great.

It was interesting to learn the past of this land. It was built in the 16th century by the Dutch. To defend their buildings during a attack from somebody, the walls of those buildings were about three feet thick. Our new partner owned a part of these buildings and opened a store to sell modern bathroom fixtures, made in Italy. When I looked a little closer, I noticed that the whole street, about one block, all the stores were selling the same thing. I was explained, that all the stores in the next street were selling different products. So, all the streets had names, that referred to the products that were sold in a particular street. So, the name of her street was called: Faucets Ave. When I asked why that was this way, they told me, that this city was the only bigger town at the whole island and when people needed some new faucets' for their home, they just had to asked for the Faucets Ave. If somebody wanted auto parts, they could got to the "Auto parts" Ave.

Even though the official language at this island was English, but mostly an home like language was spoken. It was a very small show and at the second day, we had a visit from the American Ambassador. Noticing, that the products we were offering coming from the states, he stopped at our booth and him and I had nice long talk. He himself had a need for our products and the next day somebody from the Embassy came and purchased a full box.

The show was all fun and I had always a lot of people watching my demonstration. At the same time, I had a chance to listen to original modern African music, that was played in the booth next to me. Our partner had two children and the younger girl, noticing my interest, gave me a CD with that music, as a present.

The last day of my visit, She drove me around the island and showed me many beaches and we went through some of the mountains. I noticed, that the majority of the hotels, were all American. When we said good bye, I got a big hug from everybody I made contact with. Since they all had names I couldn't pronounce, I gave them all American names and they loved it. I left with an happy: "Goodbye, see you next year."

Now I had a different experience behind me. This islands population was about one million and was a mixture of all kind of races. All of the religions were present there. The first time I had a encounter with the Islamic world. Not only was it the first time I heard the voice of the early announcer through loud speakers that came from a nearby Moshe. Saw people going to their place of worship a few times a day. When at the show I saw a fully clad woman, only her eyes were exposed, I was Spell bound and just looked at her.

This was a very seldom occurrence and when I went after her and ask her escort, if I could take a picture, it was refused, even though, I was told, that they had no problems with any of the religions. Well, I was eager to learn all these things, and it made me happy.

The following year I concentrated more on the South American countries, when I got a letter from the American Embassy in Mauritius, asking me if it would be o.k. with me to open the next "America Week" with a welcome speech. This opening greeted call the visitors that came mostly from Asia, because the Island was considered the "Gateway to Africa." Most of the references that were shown at that display, referred to the American companies, located in the country of South Africa, with their main capitol of Johannesburg. When I compared that date with the date I had of the next show at the island, they were only three days apart. So, I gave them the o.k. At the next show in Chicago, I had a very good lead in the country of Brazil. A young couple, she was raised in the US, her husband was living in his native country and had just married.

CHAPTER 21

· ·

Going to paradise?

She had just made her bar examine to become a lawyer and created a partnership with her husband. Their work consisted of waterproofing buildings, especially hotels along the Atlantic coast line. We had some meetings in the states and after they agreed upon our conditions, we set up a date, to come to them and attend their upcoming show in a city called Recife. They notified me of the receipt of their order and told me the date of the show.

I prepared myself accordingly and showed up in Brazil two days before the show. The hotel they reserved for me, was not the same they had booked for them self's. So, when we setup a morning pick up time, I made myself present at the main entrance, laden with some of our displays. After one hour, nobody showed up. I was wondering about that, but I thought, that they had encountered some problem. Finally after thirty more minutes her husband came and waved me into his car. Since this car was very small, I had a hard time to pack my stuff in it. When I was sitting next to him, he didn't say much and drove to their hotel.

When we got there, he asked me to take a seat. I did and it took a long time for them to show up. O.K. happy to see them, we drove to the show building, not too far away.

Our booth was already set up and just needed the little things I had with me. When I told them, that I waited a long time for them to pick me up, there was no follow up conversation. I ignored this situation and went to my demonstration table.

The day went by and I had a lot of fun with my visitors, especially the kids which noted my funny faces I created with my tools into the wood.

Since the show started late in the afternoon, we had to work a long afternoon and evening, before the show closed down. We went then to a nice restaurant and when they noticed, I ordered something very light, they urged me to order something heavy. When I explained to them, that I didn't eat heavy that late at night, they shook their heads and told me, that it was custom in their country to go out late at night and have a hearty meal. After they excepted my reasoning, we all went to our hotels and had a good night of sleep.

After we had set up a new pickup time in the morning, with the advice from me, not to let me wait that long again, I took that time to enjoy myself at their pool. When my time came, I went down to the entrance again and here again, they let me wait again. This time not so long, but long enough to make me feel uncomfortable. When he came again alone, he took me to their hotel again and said, that they would be down shortly, I enjoyed watching a children's TV program and when nobody showed up after a half hour, I stopped enjoying the program and started walking around. It was not, that we didn't have enough time to go to the show, I just thought it was not very polite to have me sitting there like a little kid.

Finally, they came out of the elevator when I walked over to her and told her very friendly but very determent, the I was not willing to be handled like a teenager. I told her, that I had the feeling that I was not important to her life and that made me feel uncomfortable. Her face darkened and she started to apologize by telling me, that it was kind of customary for the Brazilians, to be late. I noticed that she was very embarrassed in this situation and I told her, that I was not familiar with that and I would considered it for the next time. After a while, everything was o.k. and we concentrated our self's on the show and it went well and we made good sales.

After a few weeks, they sent in another order and everybody seemed to be happy. The second order went out and right after that I got a message from them, that they could not buy from us anymore, because the Brazilian government blocked the import from a foreign country. I was very sad to hear that, because in the meantime he had increased his customer base and all three of us had established a nice relationship.

The time for my next trip to the island of Mauritius had come and I left myself plenty of time for my trip, because I still had to meet my rep in Germany to see some of his new leads. One day, when we were done visiting customers and we just crossed the border from Holland to Germany, when my rep turned on the radio. After he found his favored station, the only thing we could her was a hefty screaming and I thought at first, that that screaming was one of the new modern songs. When I listened a little bit closer, I heard the voice of a American reporter yelling with a very nervous voice, something about air planes flying into a building in New York. It took me a few minutes to understand what was going on. My rep didn't understand what was said and I screamed at him and told him what was going on. Of course from that moment we only listened to that station. Just like my face he had a big question look on his face.

When he dropped me off my hotel and I turned on the TV of course I saw the whole debacle right in front of me. It didn't take too long when my phone was ringing and my wife was on the phone. She was very frightened und urged me to come home right away. Since we lived very close to O'Hare airport, she noticed, no airplanes were flying and the streets were all empty.

I told her, to call her the next morning to get more details. I did and we knew more now and there were some cars on the street and some airplanes were flying again. So, she was o.k. by herself. I had to spend some days in Germany, to visit new accounts and of course everybody spoke about New York.

When the day for my extension flight to the island arrived, everybody had settled down a bit. Immediately, when I came to the airport however, I noticed a different atmosphere. A lot more police and dogs were around. At that moment I felt like being back in East Germany. I had no problems and in time I was guided in my airplane seat.

After another grueling never ending flight, I arrived in the middle of the night. However, I was notified of that, through an email. An extra car with driver was waiting for me and he took me to a new hotel, directly located next to a bay, that was touching the city. It was a new section and was distinctive from the city. My hotel was right in the middle of it and faced the ocean. I had a awful night of sleep and got up early enough, not to miss the American Week beginning. This was held in the same hotel. After I found the appropriate room, I stepped in and noticed a room with a angled floor. It was higher in the back. It was lined up with a lot rows of seats.

The first three rows were occupied, so I had to go to the fourth row. Not long after I sat down, the door opened again and the American ambassador arrived. After we sat down again, the ambassador stepped behind the pedestal and started to great all the people. This was a closed meeting, reserved for only invited guests. Once he was done with the welcome speech, he then begun to introduce every one. Among these people, I heard the name of their companies, like Motorola, IBM, Boeing, Xerox etc. All of these companies had their main offices in Johannesburg. None of the persons introduced, were from the US. When he arrived on my name and introduced me not only by my name, but also mentioned, that I was a native of Chicago, everybody looked at me. For a few seconds there was no movement in the room, until a gentleman stood up, stepped up to me, stretched his hand out to me, grabbed my hand and said: "Dear Sir, please tell all Americans, that we are very sorry about what happened in New York and that we condemn that action from the bottom of our hearts. Our thoughts are with them." He then turned around and went back to his place, when suddenly, all these people, one after another, stepped up to me, shook my hand and said: "We are sorry." Of course, I had to control my emotions. When they were all done and went back to their seats, I was then motioned by the Ambassador to come down and hold my welcome speech. Of course, I was prepared for that and started. Everybody paid very close attention to what I had to say. When I was finished, they gave me a big hand and were asking, what company I was representing. Of course, I couldn't help myself to lifting my voice a bit and announced the name of it.

The last part of that day, after I said hello to my dealer, who had come to see me right after the meeting. I was physically not capable to do anything and went up to my room and had a very good night sleep. The next morning the show started and after a while, the mayor of the Island came around to every single exhibitor and greeted him or her. His microphone was set, so his words were transmitted to all the speakers in the hall. When he came to our booth, he started talking to my dealer. She was a well known business woman and collected a lot of recognition by the people.

When he was done with her, he stepped over to me, asked me for my name and explained to the people who I was and where I came from. I heard again an applause, that lasted for a while. My spirit was up and I felt good about being an American. In the meantime, I had supported my old time customers in Europe and in Asia. Sales went up and when I left my company for retirement, I felt good inside, because not only had I increased the export sales tremendously, but had learned a lot. I had seen the world and my wife participated as much as she could.

Many times I met people, that had nothing but their enthusiasm. Their countries were just coming out of the bushes and many of their people didn't even know about some countries they were now visiting. At one time, I had a couple of people coming from Palestine. Their English was not very good, but they wanted to do business with us. They had to fight the Israeli government and under very difficult circumstances they finally got the o.k. and we could sent out an order. The circumstances we had to work with were much higher in costs, then the whole order was.

But I felt good about it. Many months later, I got a picture of the work they had done with our materials and I was very humbled to see people that were happy with little things in life. I never heard from them again, but I told that story over and over again.

CHAPTER 22

· ·

Conclusion!

Is there a perfect salesman? With a clear conscience I can say: I don't think so. If there were, that man would be in competition with his colleagues, because he would be an outsider. I have seen all kind of sales people. Some that talked too much and talked to them selv's out of an order. I have seen salespeople, that didn't talk enough and didn't get an order, or I have seen salesmen starting a fight about commission, right in front of customers, who turned around and left and I have seen sales people, that, after every sentence start a short laugh, (With women we call it "Giggling") whether it's funny or not. This can be very annoying.

I have met sales people, that had no respect for their peers. On one day at the Chicago show, I noticed a middle aged woman, commonly clad and did not show a friendly face. She was looking at our booth and at one point, she walked over to me and asked me, pointing at my export partners, who had all just arrived, if those were all the export dealers we had. I nodded my head and said: "Yes just about." She then turned to them and started talking to them. When all of my guys were listening to her, one turned to me and shrugged his shoulders. That was a sign for me to come over. When I went there, she told me, that she was trying to get these people to sell her products in there respected countries When I looked at her and then the guys, I said.: "That's up to you." They all rejected her. Because, here I could tell, that that woman had the impertinence to go over the head of our president an ignored me as the export manager, to do business with our people. She also ignored, that these people, mostly young and hard working, deserved respect, by letting them know beforehand of her visit. They deserved some time to think about it. They were leading their businesses sometimes under very harsh circum-stances. Everybody knows, how expensive it is to open up foreign countries.

She thought she cut take a short cut, which was actually a good thought, but she took the wrong way and came out with nothing.

Any salesman can work as hard as he can, there will always be situations, when in negotiations for a contract, verbal or written, two minutes or two months, one or the other party makes a mistake and the whole deal goes down.

I have had it a couple of times that a mistake was made by the back office. At one time, our finance department, who got a application by the customer, for credit. It was denied for the reason, his credit rating was too low. When the customer objected to that vehemently, the office took its time and after a few weeks, they found out, that they made a mistake. The credit rating of that company was actually one of the highest. When I called my customer, to tell him about this, his assistant talked to me and told me, that they had gone to another company. Of course, a mistake like that, always reflects on the salesman's record.

Or when a customer from Israel had given me an half container size order, and after he paid, he increased that order by a little, and than being told, that they could not include that increase, because he had to pay first. The customer than told me, that he would pay the bill immediately after he arrived at his office overseas. This was rejected by the office and the customer got very irritated. I never heard from him again. The efforts, me and him put in over a few months of negotiations, were down the tube. Even though this was not my fault, but I could always feel the looks I got from the office.

Sometimes I had a customer talking to us about an order over and over again, when I got to the point of frustration and I saw no progress, I just dropped him, because after all that talking, this customer sounded like trouble. I recalled that moment in Germany, when many years ago, a successful salesman told me, don't do business with a unhappy customer, he'll be nothing but trouble.

There were many things I had learned as a young man, back at the time, when I was eager to be a good salesman, I carried with me all my life.

Now, at the end of career, I was blessed to represent a solid company, with good principals, with a solid financial base, and a motto: Customers and our working people first, made my working for them a pleasure. Because of that and my enthusiasm, made it profitable for my company. I was very proud to serve our "Big Mac" and felt bad, after he left his office and went into retirement. The company got a new president and a couple of years later, I decided also to retire.

When I look back on my whole life, I am a happy man now and even my wife, who passed away a few years ago, would agree with me.

The End!

www.ingramcontent.com/pod-product-compliance
Lightning Source LLC
Chambersburg PA
CBHW022113170526
45157CB00004B/1612